CW00693764

# BRANCH LINE TO ONGAR

### J.E.Connor
#### Series Editor Vic Mitchell

MP Middleton Press

*Published August 2007*

*ISBN 978 1 906008 05 5*

*© Middleton Press, 2007*

*Cover design Deborah Esher*

*Layout and typesetting London Railway Record*

*Published by*
    *Middleton Press*
    *Easebourne Lane*
    *Midhurst*
    *West Sussex*
    *GU29 9AZ*
*Tel: 01730 813169*
*Fax: 01730 812601*
*Email: info@middletonpress.co.uk*
*www.middletonpress.co.uk*

*Printed & bound by Biddles Ltd, Kings Lynn*

# INDEX

## ACKNOWLEDGMENTS

In addition to the various photographers whose work has made this volume possible, I wish to thank Terence Atkins and Alan Simpson who kindly provided postcards and prints from their collections, along with Mark Dewell who supplied details of the present Epping Ongar Railway. I also express my gratitude to the various friends who read the proofs prior to publication, with special thanks to Ian Strugnell, whose comments proved most useful and Bryan Wilson of the SRS and GERS, who supplied much of the information on signal boxes, although I take full responsibility for any anomalies which have remained un-noticed.

## GEOGRAPHICAL SETTING

The lines are on the clays of the northern flank of the lower Thames Valley and were built through open farmland to a large extent. They were the prime cause for the urbanisation of the district in a short space of time. From a start at about 20ft above sea level, the tracks reach around 130ft near Grange Hill.

The population of Epping grew from 3,787 in 1901 to 10,070 in 1961, while Ongar reduced from 2,084 to 1,673 in the same period.

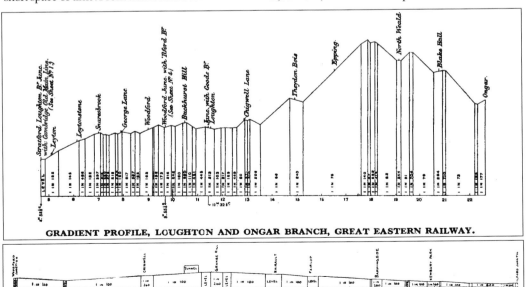

**GRADIENT PROFILE, LOUGHTON AND ONGAR BRANCH, GREAT EASTERN RAILWAY.**

GRADIENT PROFILE OF THE GREAT EASTERN RAILWAY'S NEW LINE FROM WOODFORD TO ILFORD.

The Railway Magazine

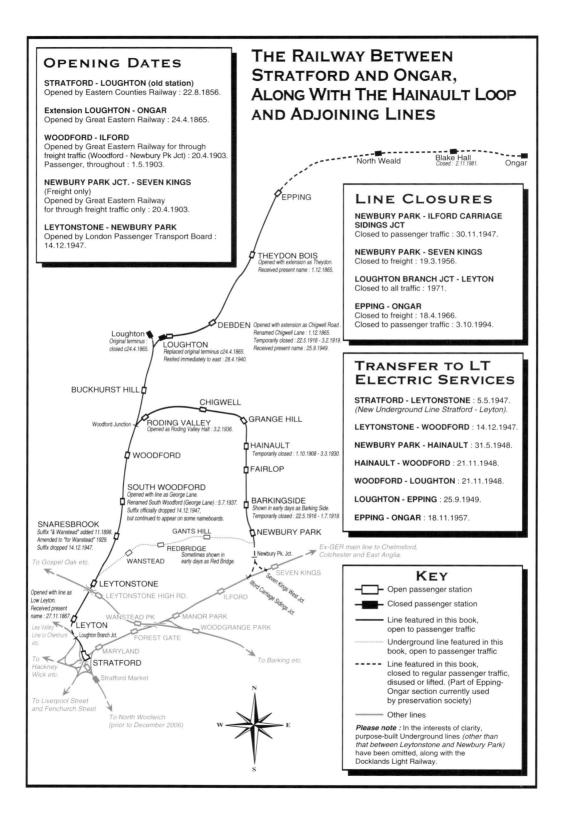

## OPENING DATES

**STRATFORD - LOUGHTON (old station)**
Opened by Eastern Counties Railway : 22.8.1856.

**Extension LOUGHTON - ONGAR**
Opened by Great Eastern Railway : 24.4.1865.

**WOODFORD - ILFORD**
Opened by Great Eastern Railway for through
freight traffic (Woodford - Newbury Pk Jct) : 20.4.1903.
Passenger, throughout : 1.5.1903.

**NEWBURY PARK JCT. - SEVEN KINGS**
(Freight only)
Opened by Great Eastern Railway
for through freight traffic only : 20.4.1903.

**LEYTONSTONE - NEWBURY PARK**
Opened by London Passenger Transport Board :
14.12.1947.

## THE RAILWAY BETWEEN STRATFORD AND ONGAR, ALONG WITH THE HAINAULT LOOP AND ADJOINING LINES

North Weald

Blake Hall
*Closed : 2.11.1981.*

Ongar

EPPING

## LINE CLOSURES

**NEWBURY PARK - ILFORD CARRIAGE
SIDINGS JCT**
Closed to passenger traffic : 30.11.1947.

**NEWBURY PARK - SEVEN KINGS**
Closed to freight : 19.3.1956.

**LOUGHTON BRANCH JCT - LEYTON**
Closed to all traffic : 1971.

**EPPING - ONGAR**
Closed to freight : 18.4.1966.
Closed to passenger traffic : 3.10.1994.

THEYDON BOIS
*Opened with extension as Theydon.
Received present name : 1.12.1865.*

Loughton
*Original terminus :
closed c24.4.1865.*

LOUGHTON
*Replaced original terminus c24.4.1865.
Resited immediately to east : 28.4.1940.*

DEBDEN *Opened with extension as Chigwell Road .
Renamed Chigwell Lane : 1.12.1865.
Temporarily closed : 22.5.1916 - 3.2.1919.
Received present name : 25.9.1949.*

## TRANSFER TO LT ELECTRIC SERVICES

**STRATFORD - LEYTONSTONE :** 5.5.1947.
*(New Underground Line Stratford - Leyton).*

**LEYTONSTONE - WOODFORD :** 14.12.1947.

**NEWBURY PARK - HAINAULT :** 31.5.1948.

**HAINAULT - WOODFORD :** 21.11.1948.

**WOODFORD - LOUGHTON :** 21.11.1948.

**LOUGHTON - EPPING :** 25.9.1949.

**EPPING - ONGAR :** 18.11.1957.

BUCKHURST HILL

CHIGWELL

Woodford Junction

RODING VALLEY
*Opened as Roding Valley Halt : 3.2.1936.*

GRANGE HILL

WOODFORD

HAINAULT
*Temporarily closed : 1.10.1908 - 3.3.1930.*

FAIRLOP

SOUTH WOODFORD
*Opened with line as George Lane.
Renamed South Woodford (George Lane) : 5.7.1937.
Suffix officially dropped 14.12.1947,
but continued to appear on some nameboards.*

BARKINGSIDE
*Shown in early days as Barking Side.
Temporarily closed : 22.5.1916 - 1.7.1919.*

SNARESBROOK
*Suffix '& Wanstead" added 11.1898.
Amended to "for Wanstead" 1929.
Suffix dropped 14.12.1947.*

GANTS HILL

NEWBURY PARK

To Gospel Oak etc.

REDBRIDGE
*Sometimes shown in
early days as Red Bridge.*

WANSTEAD

Newbury Pk. Jct.

*Ex-GER main line to Chelmsford,
Colchester and East Anglia.*

SEVEN KINGS

Seven Kings West Jct.

LEYTONSTONE

LEYTONSTONE HIGH RD.

ILFORD

Ilford Carriage Sidings Jct.

## KEY

Open passenger station

Closed passenger station

Line featured in this book,
open to passenger traffic

Underground line featured in this
book, open to passenger traffic

Line featured in this book,
closed to regular passenger traffic,
disused or lifted. (Part of Epping-
Ongar section currently used
by preservation society)

Other lines

***Please note :*** In the interests of clarity,
purpose-built Underground lines *(other than
that between Leytonstone and Newbury Park)*
have been omitted, along with the
Docklands Light Railway.

LEYTONSTONE
*Opened with line as
Low Leyton.
Received present
name : 27.11.1867.*

Lea Valley
Line to Cheshunt
etc.

WANSTEAD PK.

MANOR PARK

WOODGRANGE PARK

LEYTON
Loughton Branch Jct.

FOREST GATE

To
Hackney
Wick etc.

MARYLAND

STRATFORD

Stratford Market

To Liverpool Street
and Fenchurch Street

To North Woolwich
*(prior to December 2006)*

To Barking etc.

N
W — E
S

# HISTORICAL BACKGROUND

The London Underground Central Line route serving Epping has a history which dates back to the mid-nineteenth century.

The first scheme was proposed by the London & Blackwall Railway in 1845, but this was doomed to failure. The LBR had opened five years earlier and operated a novel system linking Fenchurch Street in the City with a Thames-side terminus at Blackwall. At the time of opening, the Company had no intention of connecting its line to any other routes, so the tracks were laid to a non-standard gauge of 5ft. In addition, to reduce the risk of fire to adjoining dock properties, the use of steam locomotives was ruled out and an ingenious, if rather unreliable, form of cable haulage was employed instead.

As the decade progressed however, the LBR was beginning to feel isolated, so the Company decided to adapt its existing line for locomotive working and build a new branch to the Essex market town of Epping.

This 1845 scheme was to diverge at Stepney, then continue to Bow, where a junction would be made with the Eastern Counties Railway linking Shoreditch with Essex and East Anglia. LBR trains would then use either ECR metals, or an adjoining line of their own, as far as Stratford, where the new route would head off in a north-easterly direction to Wanstead, Woodford, Chigwell, Loughton and Abridge, before terminating at Epping.

Not surprisingly the ECR was not keen on the idea and refused permission for the LBR to operate into Stratford. Lengthy negotiations followed and eventually the two companies agreed that the LBR could build its connecting line to Bow, but the proposed Epping branch would belong to the Eastern Counties Railway.

With the matter more or less settled, the ECR drew up a scheme whereby it would construct two routes to Epping. The chief section would diverge from the Northern & Eastern Railway to the north of Lea Bridge, then continue through Wood Street, Woodford, Loughton and Theydon Bois, before reaching its terminus at Epping. There would also be a connection, which would leave the ECR main line west of Ilford and join the branch at Woodford.

The line from Lea Bridge was deemed to threaten the fringes of Epping Forest, so it was rejected by Parliament, but the route from Ilford received the Royal Assent on 16th July 1846. The authorising Act stated that it enabled *"...the Eastern Counties Railway to make a Railway from Epping to a Point of Junction with the Colchester Line of the Eastern Counties Railway at or near the Ilford Station thereon."*

Having obtained its Bill, the ECR tried to raise the necessary capital, but sadly failed. Various changes were made to reduce expenditure, but the costs still exceeded the Company's funds and the powers for construction eventually lapsed.

A further scheme, known as the Woodford Railway, was promoted by a prominent local landowner in 1852, but, once again, this was seen by the ECR as an invasion into its territory. If it had been built, the route would have diverged from the North London line near Hackney Wick, then continued across the Lea Valley to Walthamstow and Woodford.

In opposition the ECR presented its own Bill, this time for a line linking Stratford with Loughton, more or less serving the areas included within the London & Blackwall scheme of the previous decade.

Both schemes were placed before Parliament, but it was the ECR route which ultimately succeeded and on 8th July 1853 the Royal Assent was given which enabled *"...the Eastern Counties Railway to construct a Railway from the Line of the Northern & Eastern Railway near Stratford to Woodford and Loughton."*

Within a week of the Act being passed, the ECR instructed its solicitors to arrange for the necessary land to be purchased and this time the Company met with success. The well-known George Parker Bidder was appointed as engineer whilst the construction was to be chiefly carried out by contractor, Thomas Brassey. The line was to be double-track throughout and by February 1855 it was reported that about three-quarters of the necessary land had been acquired.

Work was virtually completed by the following year and the line was inspected on behalf of the Board of Trade by the redoubtable William Yolland, then a Lieutenant-Colonel, on 13th August 1856.

Yolland noted that some signalling work remained unfinished and that a planned turntable at Loughton was still only partially built. He also added that clocks had to be provided at all the stations and refused to allow opening until the various refinements had been made. As most of these were of a comparatively minor nature, they were dealt with in a week, although it was expected that completion of the Loughton turntable would take a fortnight. Having received confirmation from the ECR that the majority of his requirements had been carried out, Yolland agreed to recommend opening, although he stipulated that only tank engines could be used until the turntable was operational.

Services commenced on Friday 22nd August 1856. According to *The Railway Times* published three days later, the line had opened *"without notice or ceremony"*.

Stations were provided at Low Leyton, Leytonstone, Snaresbrook, George Lane, Woodford, Buckhurst Hill and Loughton, with the last located east of the High Road.

Two years later, in 1858, a separate concern, known as the Epping Railways Company, made a bid to extend the line to Epping and Chipping Ongar. Around this time there was a great deal of rivalry between companies and it seems that the ER was part of a scheme which would ultimately provide the Eastern Union and Norfolk Railways with their own route into London. The Epping Railways Company was officially independent, but it is interesting that its Chairman, George Parker Bidder again, occupied the same position with the Norfolk Railway.

The ER scheme received Parliamentary authority in 1859, but before construction started, the Company acquired further powers in 1860 for the line to be extended from Chipping Ongar to Dunmow.

The Eastern Counties Railway, once again being protective of its territory, decided to block the scheme and in 1861 received powers to build a line linking Braintree and Bishops Stortford by way of Dunmow.

Such pointless and wasteful rivalries in the area came to an end in July / August 1862, when firstly the Epping Railways Company was taken over by the Eastern Counties and then the ECR, the Eastern Union and other concerns were amalgamated to form the Great Eastern Railway. The Ongar - Dunmow extension was abandoned at the same time.

The new company lost no time in starting work on the Loughton - Ongar line, and on 29th August 1862 Thomas Brassey was awarded the main contract for construction.

Because much of the area to be served was lightly populated, it was only deemed necessary to provide a single track, although passing loops were planned at both Theydon and Epping.

In order to serve Epping, the line had to feature some pretty impressive gradients and to the east of the town the formation reached a summit of 340ft above sea level. For many years this was the highest point on the GER, until the distinction passed to the Elsenham - Thaxted branch in 1913.

The Ongar line diverged from the existing route about a quarter of a mile south of the original Loughton terminus. It then headed through new stations at Loughton, Chigwell Road, Theydon, Epping, North Weald and Blake Hall before reaching its ultimate destination at Ongar.

It was inspected on behalf of the Board of Trade in the early part of April 1865 by Captain Tyler, but he found a number of items unfinished and refused to sanction opening. These were soon dealt with however and, without any advance notice, trains commenced running on Monday 24th April 1865. There was little in the way of celebrations, although *The Chelmsford Chronicle* reported that the cadet corps from a local grammar school assembled on the platform at Ongar to salute the first arrival with a rifle volley. For the rest of the day a number of passengers travelled back and forth over the line, but the party mood came to an abrupt end when the locomotive working the last down train left the rails at North Weald. There were no injuries, but passengers expecting to arrive in Ongar at 9.30pm were delayed until 5am.

With the new extension fully operational the old terminus at Loughton was closed and the land sold off.

In time, increasing traffic resulted in the formation between Loughton and Epping being doubled in 1892, but the stretch towards Ongar remained single.

## THE FAIRLOP OR HAINAULT LOOP

The growth of suburban housing around Ilford in the 1890s and the prospect of further developments to the north, brought proposals for a new line. This was promoted independently in 1895 and was to be known as the Ilford, Barkingside & Chigwell Row Railway. The GER, acting as territorially as its predecessor, sprang into action to protect its interests. The IBCRR Bill was placed before Parliament in 1896, but was subsequently withdrawn when the Great Eastern Railway undertook to promote a line to serve the area itself.

In its General Powers Act of 1897, the GER obtained permission to construct a 5mile 7furlong 7chain loop line between Ilford and Woodford by way of Barkingside and Chigwell. In addition there would be a 1.7chain eastern-facing spur at the Ilford end, so that traffic to and from East Anglia had access to the route.

The firm of C.J. Wills was employed as contractors and work commenced in 1900. It was clear that the GER was confident about the line's success, as the six intermediate stations were designed by the GER architect

Neville Ashbee to full London suburban standards.

Services, both passenger and local freight, commenced running on 1st May 1903, but the Company's optimism proved unfounded as there was in the event little development in the area served prior to 1914.

Writing in the *Railway Magazine* of December 1907, Cecil J. Allen observed that there was *"scarcely a house in sight"* of the closely spaced *"palatial"* stations at Hainault and Fairlop and that passenger figures at both *"could often be counted on the fingers"*.

Built on arches, both Hainault and Fairlop looked hopelessly out of place surrounded by empty Essex fields. Within a short while, the GER decided that the expense of retaining both of them was not justified, so Hainault station, and its attendant goods yard, was closed after traffic on 30th September 1908. Sadly this did little to improve the situation, as in 1911 it was reported that the loop was still a drain on resources.

## WORLD WAR I AND AFTER

The onset of war in 1914 resulted in various changes on both routes, including the closure of two more stations, although both of these were later reopened. An emergency hospital had been constructed to the west of the Loop Line station at Newbury Park back in 1912 and this subsequently became the destination for ambulance trains conveying wounded soldiers from the front. Fighter stations were established on Fairlop Plain, Hainault Farm and North Weald to provide air defences for London and these, together with the construction of various army camps, resulted in extra traffic.

After the war ended, railways throughout the country found themselves in a run-down physical and financial condition and this led to the Railway Grouping which took place on 1st January 1923. From that date, the majority of British main line companies became part of four major groups, with the GER being absorbed into the London & North Eastern Railway.

Under the LNER both the Ongar line and Fairlop Loop (later known as the Hainault Loop) remained much as before, although drastic changes would ultimately come. The fortunes of the Loop certainly improved during the 1930s, with the reopening of Hainault station, the construction of Roding Valley Halt and the promise of a new London airport at Fairlop, although the latter scheme never came to fruition.

Before the grouping the GER had considered electrifying parts of its suburban system, but these ideas came to nothing. The issue then passed to the LNER and, although various proposals were discussed, nothing materialised until the announcement of the London Railways New Works Programme in 1935. Among other things, this scheme envisaged the extension of the Central London tube line beyond its existing terminus at Liverpool Street in tunnel to Stratford, where surface level cross-platform interchange with LNER Shenfield services would be available. From here it would again dive under ground until joining the existing Ongar branch close to the south end of Leyton station. The rest of the route would remain largely as before, although a new underground link would diverge at Leytonstone and join the Fairlop Loop south of Newbury Park.

It was hoped that all these changes would be implemented by 1940, but once again fate stepped in and in September 1939, the country again found itself at war.

Some of the work had been completed, but much of it was deferred until hostilities ended in 1945.

One of the most notable tasks undertaken prior to the wartime suspension was the construction of a new station at Loughton, slightly east of its 1865 predecessor. This was very much in the architectural style favoured at the time and was opened, albeit in an unfinished state, on 28th April 1940.

Work on the other sections of the scheme resumed after the war and on 4th December 1946, London Passenger Transport Board tube trains were extended from Liverpool Street to Stratford. Five months later they reached Leytonstone, where the existing up platform was rebuilt as an island with the east side acting as a temporary bay for steam services to and from the Ongar direction.

Apart from the new premises at Loughton and the rebuilding of Leytonstone, the stations along the route remained much as before, although the track was raised to give a reduced platform height of 2ft 9ins for the tube stock.

On 14th December 1947, electric services were extended northwards from Leytonstone, along both the old ECR route to Woodford and the new link to Newbury Park. For a brief period Newbury Park was used as a terminus, although the conductor rails were energised through to Grange Hill so that stock could reach a new depot which had been built at Hainault back in 1939.

The following year proved to be eventful, with electrified passenger services being extended from Newbury Park to Hainault on 31st May 1948, and then from Woodford to Loughton and Hainault on 21st November. The extension of the service from Loughton to Epping came ten months later on 25th September 1949.

From then on, steam locomotives ceased to be used on regular passenger trains south of Epping, although they were retained on the push-pull shuttle service between there and Ongar. This continued to operate for a further eight years and enjoyed the benefit of a passing loop which had been added at North Weald on 14th August 1949. The steam shuttles were replaced by tube trains from 18th November 1957, which somehow looked very incongruous running through the Essex countryside.

Although the old GER link from Ilford had been made redundant by the tube extension in 1947, the line from Newbury Park via the eastern curve to Seven Kings remained open for freight traffic until 19th March 1956. Goods trains continued to work the Ongar and Fairlop lines for a further decade, but ceased completely as from 18th April 1966. The original ECR line between Leyton and Loughton Branch Junction, latterly singled,

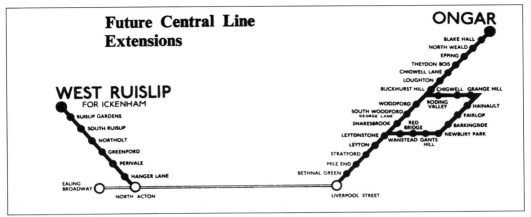

Diagram showing Central Line extensions taken from an LPTB leaflet of 1947, when electrification of the whole route to Ongar was thought to be imminent.

remained in limited use until official closure in May 1971.

Despite new housing being erected at Ongar, traffic on the section beyond Epping remained light. Blake Hall lost its Sunday services in 1966 and London Transport announced its intention to close the Epping - Ongar stretch in 1970. After much discussion, the Essex County Council agreed to subsidise the route for a quarter of its annual loss in 1976, but with services reduced the passing loop at North Weald was taken out of use.

The Council subsidy was withdrawn in 1977 and a further closure plan was announced in 1980. This again failed to be implemented, but the following year brought an end to the little used Blake Hall station, which closed after

traffic on Saturday 31st October 1981.

Trains between Epping and Ongar were reduced to operating during Monday - Friday peak periods only from 6th December 1982, but near the end of the decade, on 30th October 1989, an all week service was restored in a last ditch attempt to save the line.

Sadly this failed and the line beyond Epping closed completely after 30th September 1994. The route has since been the subject of preservation proposals and the Epping Ongar Volunteer Railway commenced operating return trips between Ongar and North Weald on Sundays from 3rd October 2005.

Elsewhere, the route which started life back in the 1850s, along with much of the Hainault Loop, both long-since rejuvenat-

# PASSENGER SERVICES

In 1856, the Eastern Counties Railway operated a total of eight trains in each direction on weekdays and six on Sundays. The majority of weekday services ran to and from the London & Blackwall Railway terminus at Fenchurch Street, but on Sundays they

used the ECR's own premises at Bishopsgate. A few trains ran as semi-fasts and these took about forty minutes to complete their journeys, whilst the remainder called at all stations and took around ten minutes longer.

Traffic grew steadily and by 1882

Loughton had thirty-seven trains each way, Epping eleven and Ongar ten. By 1889, the Loughton service had increased to forty-four each way, but the service beyond could not be enhanced until after the 1892 doubling. The 1894 timetable showed twenty trains to Epping, of which thirteen continued to Ongar.

The opening of the Fairlop Loop brought more trains to the southern section of line, resulting in Woodford having seventy-two in the down direction and sixty-seven up.

With the Loop operational, it became possible to work a more or less circular service from and to either Liverpool Street or Fenchurch Street. The trains, which were formed of four-wheel coaches, took around ninety minutes to complete the round trip, standing for a while at Fairlop before continuing their journeys.

Outside the peak periods, Loop Line services were largely reduced to working between Ilford and Woodford in late GER days, although some travelled further. On Sundays the local trains ran every hour, but the demand was so light that the number was halved in the interests of economy during World War I. The full service was restored from 1st May 1921 and, because of new housing then being erected, trains over the Fairlop Loop began to run half-hourly in 1933.

The Monday-Friday timetable of 1930-31 shows that the first train for Liverpool Street departed from Loughton at 5.05am and arrived at 5.42am, having called at all stations en-route. Passengers requiring the Fenchurch Street line could change at Stratford and arrive in the City at 5.54am. Workings from Ongar started at the more leisurely time of 7.07am, when the first train departed for Fenchurch Street. This again called at all stations and arrived at 8.28am. However, the next departure from Ongar, which left at 7.49am, was faster, as it missed out both Chigwell Lane and Buckhurst Hill, then ran non-stop between Snaresbrook and Liverpool Street, where it arrived at 8.54am.

In the opposite direction, the last train for Ongar left Liverpool Street at 9.48pm, but there were later trains for Epping at 10.46pm and 11.55pm. The final down train departed from Liverpool Street at 16 minutes past midnight, but this only went as far as Loughton. During the same period, the last through working to Loughton left Fenchurch Street at 6.40pm, but connections at Stratford were available until the 9.58pm departure, which called at all stations except Leman Street and Shadwell.

The changes brought about by electrification resulted in a service frequency which could never have been envisaged in steam days. Because Fairlop had been treated as an intermediate terminus, the route was normally referred to as the Fairlop Loop, but with the various operational changes introduced by LT it became known as the Hainault Loop.

Once the routes had been fully electrified, the main service pattern consisted of trains operated between central London and Epping or else to Hainault via Newbury Park. The Woodford - Hainault section was largely served by a shuttle and was subsequently used as a testbed for experimental automatic train operation.

British Railways locomotives and stock continued to operate the Epping-Ongar shuttles until being replaced by Underground units in 1957. This was not the end of BR passenger operation on the route however, as occasional excursion trains continued to run for a few more years. In addition to these, a handful of regular early morning trains continued to run between Stratford (weekdays) or the ex-GER terminus at Liverpool Street (Sundays) and either Loughton or Epping. These BR trains, latterly DMUs, were withdrawn on 31st May 1970, thereby enabling the junction at Leyton to be taken out of use in 1971.

# STRATFORD

The original Stratford station stood to the west of Angel Lane and was opened by the Eastern Counties Railway on 20th June 1839. Two further platforms were added to serve the Northern & Eastern Railway route to Broxbourne which opened on 15th September 1840, but these lay west of the earlier premises and were regarded as completely separate. Within a few years however, it was decided to move the Colchester line platforms further west and undertake other alterations so the two stations could be combined into one. The enlarged premises were brought into use on 1st April 1847 and the 1839 buildings in Angel Lane were closed. A passenger subway linking all platforms was provided in 1876. In 1886-7, new station and platform buildings were provided, and an additional entrance was opened in Martin Street. The up local platform was converted into an island in 1898, so that it could also serve the down Through line and, in the same year, the station was officially renamed 'Stratford (West Ham)' although the suffix does not seem to have been used consistently. An additional platform for up Through line trains was added beside a new up side loop in 1900 and twenty-three years later, soon after the grouping the bracketed suffix 'West Ham' was dropped from the station's name.

1. We start our journey with this view of the main entrance to Stratford station, as it appeared around 1914. It was located in the angle between platforms 4 and 5 (now 10A and 11) and was reached from the west side of Angel Lane by means of an approach known as Station Road. The replacement building seen here was erected in 1886-7, but in the event its usage soon declined, as the Martin Street entrance proved more popular, and it finally closed to passengers from 23rd October 1944. Much of the building remained standing in 2007, although it had long since been reduced to a derelict shell. (J.F. Gairns)

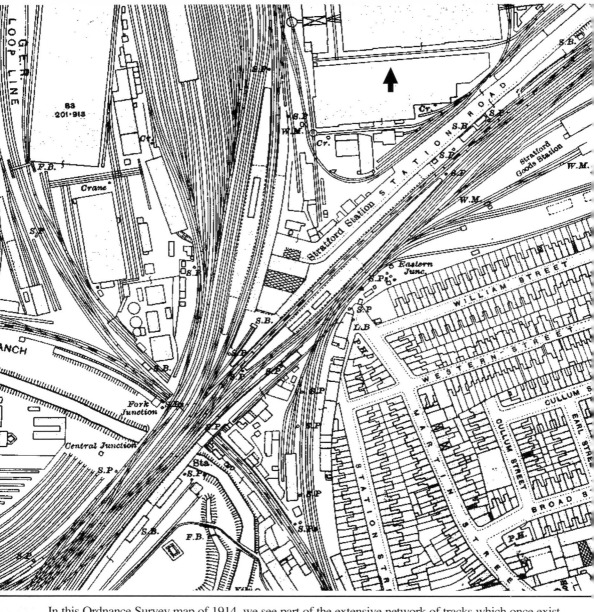

In this Ordnance Survey map of 1914, we see part of the extensive network of tracks which once existed around Stratford. The main line is that which crosses diagonally from bottom left to top right, whilst the route serving Ongar and the Lea Valley diverges northwards. At this time, the high level station comprised seven platform faces, which were numbered from south to north, with Number 1 serving the loop added in 1900. Station Road, which provided access to the main entrance, can be seen near the top right, leading down from Angel Lane and adjoining the rear wall of Platform 4. Above this lies part of the GER locomotive works, which had been established in 1847 to replace an earlier plant near Romford. The sidings to the left of the Ongar and Lea Valley line platforms served carriage facilities, whilst west of these lay further locomotive shops and the running shed complex. The two sets of lines coming together to form a vee at the base of the map head south towards Beckton, North Woolwich and the Royal Albert Docks. That to the left is the passenger route, which includes the platforms of Stratford Low Level, whilst to the right lies the Eastern Curve, which dated from 1847 and was intended for freight traffic only. A little to the east of this curve is Martin Street, which leads up to the south side station entrance of 1886.

2.   Standing on platform 1 in the 1930s, we look north and see an up train from the Ongar line about to depart for the City. The short stub of track between platforms 4 and 5 was a carriage dock, and behind this lies the Stratford Timekeepers' Box. (Milepost 92½ collection)

3.   Platform 6 provides us with a good location to view an ex-GER 2-4-2T drifting in with a train from the Ongar line, again in the 1930s. Behind can be seen the works offices, whilst to the right, near the north end of platform 5, a solitary art-deco styled poster promotes the A4 pacific-hauled 'West Riding Limited'.   (Milepost 92½ collection)

4. As part of the scheme to electrify the Shenfield route and extend LPTB Central Line services into Essex, Stratford station needed to be enlarged. Two new island platforms, with bays at the London end, were provided to the south of the existing formation and are seen on the right of this photograph dating from 1949. They were still numbered from south to north, although because the sequence now started with the Low Level station, those on the High Level commenced with No. 3. Of the newly constructed section, platforms 4 and 7 were the bays intended to accommodate a shuttle service of electric trains to and from Fenchurch Street, but this failed to materialise and the link between Bow Junction and Gas Factory Junction closed to passengers instead. The old island which had previously formed platforms 2 and 3 lost its southernmost face and became No. 9. The platforms served by Ongar and Lea Valley trains were renumbered 11, 12 and 13, the last pair being the down island platform which until then had been designated 6 and 7. In this view, an ex-LMSR Class 3F 'Jinty' 0-6-0T can be seen alongside platform 11 with a freight train, possibly from the yard at Temple Mills. Immediately to the right of the locomotive stands Stratford power signal box, which was commissioned on 4th September 1949 and abolished on 6th April 1999. (British Rail)

5. After the bulk of services between Stratford and Leytonstone were taken over by the LPTB Central Line on 5th May 1947, trains calling at platforms 11, 12 and 13 were largely restricted to those serving the Lea Valley Line. The island forming platforms 12 and 13 subsequently fell into complete disuse and was partially demolished, but although stripped of its coping and buildings, it retained a white-on-blue vitreous enamel nameboard at its northern end into the 1980s. With the majority of Lea Valley traffic routed via Clapton and Copper Mill Junction, the only services using No. 11 were those which operated to and from Tottenham Hale during peak periods, as seen here, and even these ceased in July 1985. (I. Baker)

6. Since they commenced operation, westbound Central Line services have used platform 3, whilst those travelling in the opposite direction have called at No. 6. Here we see an eastbound working for Loughton, formed of 1962 Stock, ascending into the station in 1992, with the over-grown trackbed of unused bay No.7 on the right. Although this has never been served by trains, the other bay, No.4, was eventually provided with track and was used by the Docklands Light Railway from 1987 until 2007, when replaced by new purpose-built DLR platforms to the south of the formation. At the opposite end of the station, the Central Line descends back into tunnel and follows a similar course to the original route towards Leyton. (G.W. Goslin)

7. As part of the scheme to extend the London Underground Jubilee Line to Stratford, the station was furnished with a new entrance building and concourse. This provides access to all platforms and is seen as it appeared in 2007. The first stage of the Jubilee Line Extension was brought into public use between Stratford and North Greenwich on 14th May 1999, with the remaining stretch to Green Park opening in stages later in the year. (C.D. Connor)

8. Platform 12 was subsequently renovated and some remedial work was carried out on No.11. Regular passenger services between Stratford and Tottenham Hale were reintroduced on 12th December 2005, largely to provide a link to and from Stansted Airport. Here we stand at the south end of platform 12 and see the rear of a train about to depart for Stansted. Stratford continues to grow as a railway centre with a new International station opening nearby in November 2007. (I. Baker)

# NORTH OF STRATFORD

From Stratford, trains using the original alignment towards Ongar curved northwards and passed the complex of railway workshops, sheds and sidings before diverging at Loughton Branch Junction. This diagram, produced by the Railway Clearing House in 1915, shows our line diverging *"to Woodford"* at the top. The old GER route between Stratford Low Level and North Woolwich, seen at the bottom, just right of centre, closed after 9th December 2006, as part of the formation was required for an extension of the Docklands Light Railway.

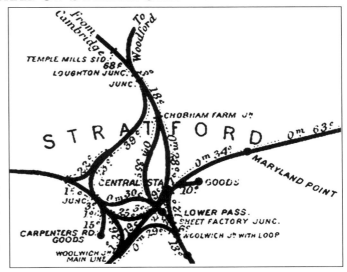

9. Little seems to have been recorded about the earliest signal box at Loughton Branch Junction, but the second cabin, which we see here, stood on the up side and was brought into use during 1879. Initially it comprised forty-six levers, but the number was increased to sixty-seven ten years later. In 1908 a new ninety-one lever frame was provided by McKenzie & Holland. This view was taken on 14th November 1954, after the box had been fitted with external supporting timbers to counteract subsidence. The box was closed from 29th June 1958 and was subsequently demolished. (P.J. Kelley)

**Other albums featuring Stratford are *Liverpool Street to Ilford* and *Branch Lines Around North Woolwich*.**

# WOODFORD BRANCH.

Trains run between Fenchurch Street, Bishopsgate, and Loughton as under:—

| Miles from Fench. St. | Down Trains. | WEEK DAYS. | | | | | | | | | | SUNDAYS—From Bishopsgate only | | | | | | | |
|---|---|---|---|---|---|---|---|---|---|---|---|---|---|---|---|---|---|---|---|
| | | 1 2 3 | 1 2 3 | 1 2 3 | 1 2 3 Par. | 1 2 | 1 2 | 1 2 3 | 1 2 3 | | | 1 2 3 Par | 1 2 3 | 1 2 3 | 1 2 3 | 1 2 3 | 1 2 3 | | |
| | FROM | mor | mor | mor. | evn. | evn. | evn. | evn. | evn. | | | mor. | evn. | evn. | evn. | evn. | evn. | | |
| — | **FENCHURCH ST.** | 8 10 | 9 10 | 10 10 | 12 10 | 4 10 | 5 10 | 6 10 | 8 40 | .. | .. | .. | .. | .. | .. | .. | .. | .. | .. |
| — | Stepney | 8 15 | 9 15 | 10 15 | 12 15 | 4 15 | .. | 6 15 | 8 45 | .. | .. | .. | .. | .. | .. | .. | .. | .. | .. |
| — | **BISHOPSGATE** | .. | .. | 10 5 | 12 7 | .. | .. | .. | .. | .. | .. | 9 45 | 2 0 | 3 0 | 4 30 | 7 15 | 8 30 | .. | .. |
| — | Mile End | .. | .. | 10 8 | 12 10 | .. | .. | .. | .. | .. | .. | 9 50 | 2 5 | 3 5 | 4 33 | 7 18 | 8 35 | .. | .. |
| 4¼ | Stratford | 8 25 | 9 25 | 10 25 | 12 25 | 4 25 | 5 25 | 6 25 | 8 55 | .. | .. | 10 5 | 2 20 | 3 20 | 4 45 | 7 30 | 8 50 | .. | .. |
| 5¼ | Low Leyton | .. | 9 30 | 10 30 | 12 30 | 4 30 | .. | 6 29 | 9 0 | .. | .. | 10 12 | 2 27 | 3 27 | 4 50 | 7 35 | 8 57 | .. | .. |
| 6¼ | Leytonstone | 8 31 | 9 34 | 10 34 | 12 31 | 4 31 | .. | 6 34 | 9 4 | .. | .. | 10 17 | 2 32 | 3 32 | 4 55 | 7 40 | 9 2 | .. | .. |
| 7¼ | Snaresbrook | .. | 9 39 | 10 39 | 12 39 | 4 39 | 5 33 | 6 39 | 9 9 | .. | .. | 10 22 | 2 37 | 3 37 | 5 0 | 7 45 | 9 7 | .. | .. |
| 8¼ | George Lane | 8 36 | 9 43 | 10 43 | 12 43 | 4 43 | 5 37 | 6 41 | 9 13 | .. | .. | 10 27 | 2 42 | 3 42 | 5 5 | 7 50 | 9 12 | .. | .. |
| 9¼ | Woodford | 8 40 | 9 48 | 10 48 | 12 48 | 4 48 | 5 42 | 6 44 | 9 18 | .. | .. | 10 32 | 2 47 | 3 47 | 5 10 | 7 55 | 9 17 | .. | .. |
| 10¾ | Buckhurst Hill | .. | 9 53 | 10 53 | 12 53 | 4 53 | .. | 6 49 | 9 23 | .. | .. | 10 37 | 2 52 | 3 52 | 5 17 | 8 2 | 9 22 | .. | .. |
| 12 | **LOUGHTON** | 8 50 | 10 0 | 11 0 | 1 0 | 5 0 | 5 50 | 6 55 | 9 30 | .. | .. | 10 45 | 3 0 | 4 0 | 5 25 | 8 10 | 9 30 | .. | .. |

| Miles from Loughton. | Up Trains. | WEEK DAYS. | | | | | | | | | | SUNDAYS—To Bishopsgate only. | | | | | | | |
|---|---|---|---|---|---|---|---|---|---|---|---|---|---|---|---|---|---|---|---|
| | | 1 2 3 | 1 2 | 1 2 | 1 2 3 | 1 2 3 | 1 2 3 | 1 2 3 | 1 2 3 Par. | | | 1 2 3 Par. | 1 2 3 | 1 2 3 | 1 2 3 | 1 2 3 | 1 2 3 | | |
| | FROM | mor | mor. | mor. | mor. | evn. | evn. | evn. | evn. | | | mor. | evn. | evn | evn. | evn. | evn | | |
| — | **LOUGHTON** | 7 10 | 8 10 | 9 12 | 11 10 | 3 10 | 4 10 | 5 10 | 7 40 | .. | .. | 8 30 | 12 40 | 3 20 | 5 45 | 7 0 | 8 31 | .. | .. |
| 1¼ | Buckhurst Hill | 7 15 | 8 14 | .. | 11 15 | 3 15 | 4 15 | 5 15 | 7 45 | .. | .. | 8 35 | 12 45 | 3 25 | 5 50 | 7 6 | 8 36 | .. | .. |
| 2¼ | Woodford | 7 18 | 8 18 | 9 22 | 11 19 | 3 19 | 4 19 | 5 19 | 7 49 | .. | .. | 8 40 | 12 50 | 3 30 | 5 56 | 7 11 | 8 41 | .. | .. |
| 3¼ | George Lane | 7 22 | 8 22 | 9 26 | 11 23 | 3 23 | 4 23 | 5 23 | 7 53 | .. | .. | 8 45 | 12 54 | 3 34 | 6 1 | 7 16 | 8 46 | .. | .. |
| 4¼ | Snaresbrook | 7 26 | 8 26 | 9 30 | 11 27 | 3 27 | 4 27 | 5 27 | 7 57 | .. | .. | 8 50 | 12 58 | 3 38 | 6 6 | 7 21 | 8 51 | .. | .. |
| 5¼ | Leytonstone | 7 30 | 8 30 | .. | 11 31 | 3 31 | 4 31 | 5 31 | 8 1 | .. | .. | 8 55 | 1 2 | 3 42 | 6 11 | 7 26 | 8 56 | .. | .. |
| 6¼ | Low Leyton | 7 34 | 8 34 | .. | 11 35 | 3 35 | 4 35 | 5 35 | 8 5 | .. | .. | 9 0 | 1 6 | 3 46 | 6 16 | 7 31 | 9 1 | .. | .. |
| 7¾ | Stratford | 7 40 | 8 40 | 9 40 | 11 40 | 3 40 | 4 40 | 5 40 | 8 10 | .. | .. | 9 10 | 1 12 | 3 52 | 6 25 | 7 40 | 9 10 | .. | .. |
| 10¾ | Mile End | .. | .. | .. | .. | .. | .. | .. | 8 30 | .. | .. | 9 23 | 1 25 | 4 0 | 6 38 | 7 53 | 9 23 | .. | .. |
| 11¾ | **BISHOPSGATE** | .. | 9 0 | .. | .. | .. | .. | 5 55 | 8 35 | .. | .. | 9 30 | 1 32 | 4 5 | 6 45 | 8 0 | 9 30 | .. | .. |
| — | Stepney | 7 50 | 8 50 | 9 50 | 11 50 | 3 50 | 4 50 | 5 50 | 8 20 | .. | .. | .. | .. | .. | .. | .. | .. | .. | .. |
| 12 | **FENCHURCH ST.** | 7 58 | 8 58 | 9 58 | 11 58 | 3 58 | 4 58 | 5 58 | 8 28 | . | . | .. | .. | .. | .. | .. | .. | .. | .. |

The Trains on Sundays will run to and from Bishopsgate only.
On Week Days Passengers from Bishopsgate and the Branch Stations require to change Carriages at Stratford.

## FARES:

| | FROM LONDON. | | | | |
|---|---|---|---|---|---|
| | SINGLE. | | | DAY. | |
| | First Class. | Second Class. | Third Class. | First Class. | Second Class. |
| | s. d. | s. d. | s. d. | s. d. | s. d. |
| Fenchurch Street | .. | .. | .. | .. | .. |
| Stepney | .. | .. | .. | .. | .. |
| Bishopsgate | .. | .. | .. | .. | .. |
| Mile End | .. | .. | .. | .. | .. |
| Stratford | 0 6 | 0 4 | 0 4 | 0 9 | 0 6 |
| Low Leyton | 0 8 | 0 6 | 0 5 | 1 0 | 0 9 |
| Leytonstone | 1 0 | 0 9 | 0 6 | 1 6 | 1 2 |
| Snaresbrook | 1 3 | 1 0 | 0 7 | 1 9 | 1 6 |
| George Lane | 1 3 | 1 0 | 0 8 | 1 9 | 1 6 |
| Woodford | 1 6 | 1 0 | 0 9 | 2 3 | 1 6 |
| Buckhurst Hill | 1 9 | 1 3 | 0 10 | 2 6 | 2 0 |
| Loughton | 2 0 | 1 6 | 1 0 | 3 0 | 2 3 |

| | FROM LOUGHTON. | | | | |
|---|---|---|---|---|---|
| | SINGLE. | | | DAY. | |
| | First Class. | Second Class. | Third Class. | First Class. | Second Class. |
| | s. d. | s. d. | s. d. | s. d. | s. d. |
| Loughton | .. | .. | .. | .. | .. |
| Buckhurst Hill | 0 3 | 0 2 | 0 1 | 0 6 | 0 3 |
| Woodford | 0 5 | 0 3 | 0 2 | 0 8 | 0 5 |
| George Lane | 0 7 | 0 5 | 0 3 | 0 11 | 0 8 |
| Snaresbrook | 0 9 | 0 6 | 0 4 | 1 3 | 0 9 |
| Leytonstone | 0 11 | 0 7 | 0 5 | 1 4 | 1 0 |
| Low Leyton | 1 1 | 0 9 | 0 6 | 1 6 | 1 3 |
| Stratford | 1 6 | 1 2 | 0 8 | 2 3 | 1 9 |
| Mile End | 2 0 | 1 6 | 1 0 | 3 0 | 2 3 |
| Bishopsgate | 2 0 | 1 6 | 1 0 | 3 0 | 2 3 |
| Stepney | 2 0 | 1 6 | 1 0 | 3 0 | 2 3 |
| Fenchurch Street | 2 0 | 1 6 | 1 0 | 3 0 | 2 3 |

## RATES FOR PERIODICAL TICKETS.

| Miles | Between London (Fenchurch Street) | FIRST CLASS.—MONTHS. | | | | | SECOND CLASS.—MONTHS. | | | | |
|---|---|---|---|---|---|---|---|---|---|---|---|
| | | 12 | 6 | 3 | 2 | 1 | 12 | 6 | 3 | 2 | 1 |
| | AND | £ s. d. | £ s. d. | £ s. d. | £ s. d. | £ s. d. | £ s. d. | £ s. d. | £ s. d. | £ s. d. | £ s. d. |
| 5¼ | Low Leyton | 13 0 0 | 8 0 0 | 4 5 0 | 2 17 6 | 1 10 0 | 9 0 0 | 5 10 0 | 3 5 0 | 2 5 0 | 1 5 0 |
| 6¼<br>7¼ | Leytonstone<br>Snaresbrook | 15 0 0 | 10 0 0 | 5 2 6 | 3 7 6 | 1 15 0 | 10 10 0 | 6 5 0 | 4 0 0 | 2 15 0 | 1 10 0 |
| 8¼<br>9¼ | George Lane<br>Woodford | 16 0 0 | 10 10 0 | 6 0 0 | 3 17 6 | 2 0 0 | 11 0 0 | 6 10 0 | 4 5 0 | 3 0 0 | 1 12 6 |
| 10¾ | Buckhurst Hill | 17 10 0 | 11 0 0 | 6 5 0 | 4 5 0 | 2 5 0 | 13 10 0 | 7 10 0 | 5 0 0 | 3 7 6 | 1 15 0 |
| 12 | Loughton | 20 0 0 | 12 8 0 | 7 10 0 | 5 10 0 | 3 3 0 | 16 0 0 | 9 10 0 | 6 0 0 | 4 5 0 | 2 5 0 |

When two or more of the same family subscribe at the same time for the same period, and to the same Station, a deduction from the above Rates will be made on the following scale:—When Two subscribe 10 per cent. reduction. When Three or more subscribe 15 per cent. reduction. Children under 14 years of age to be charged Half-price.

Applications for Season Tickets to be addressed to Mr. DAVIS, Treasurer, Bishopsgate Station.

September 1856 (A.D. Simpson collection)

# LEYTON

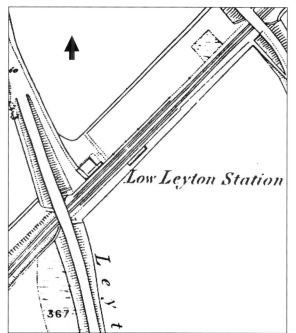

The station opened on 22nd August 1856 and was originally named 'Low Leyton'. It comprised two short platforms and, according to GER information published in 1922, was located 1mile 5chains from Stratford. It received its present name on 27th November 1867 and had its down platform extended by 150ft around 1869, following a complaint from a passenger who had met with an accident while boarding or alighting from a train. On 18th June 1873 the Way & Works Committee minutes stated the up platform was also to be lengthened. This extract from the First Edition Ordnance Survey of around 1865 shows that even after the best part of a decade since opening, the station was still surrounded by open fields.

10.  Originally tickets were purchased at platform level, but in May 1878, the GER Way & Works Committee agreed that a replacement overhead booking office should be erected on the east side of Leyton High Road. Further improvements took place in 1879, but, as the local population expanded, the facilities soon proved inadequate, so in June 1888 the company sanctioned a more substantial reconstruction. This view shows the 1888 street level building as it appeared in the early years of the twentieth century, with West Ham Corporation tramcar No. 37 pausing to pick up a lady passenger. (Commercial postcard / A.D. Simpson collection)

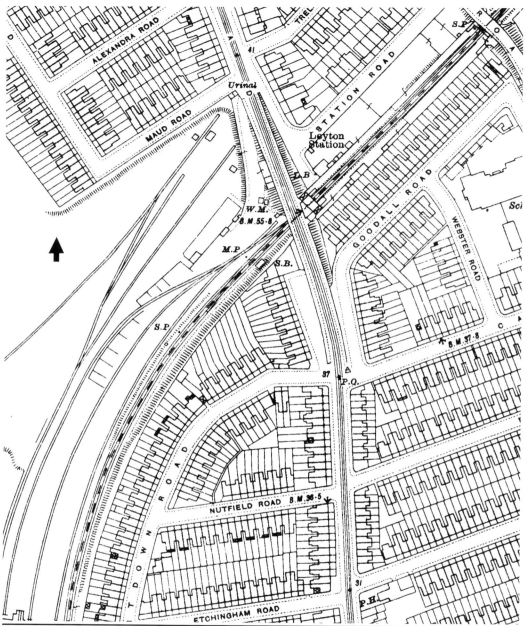

By 1914, the surrounding area had become completely developed and the green fields of yore faded into a distant memory. The station can be seen a little to the right of centre, with its main entrance on the east side of Leyton High Road. By this time however, there was also an entrance at the opposite end, which faced onto the south side of Union Road. A booking office building with a stairway link to the up platform had been provided here as part of the 1888 improvements. The lengthy canopies on both sides also dated from 1888. To the left of the map lies the goods yard, which was brought into use in 1887. Part of the yard was later occupied by an engineers' depot used by the Permanent Way Department.

11. A variety of hats abound as commuters prepare to board an incoming up train in the early part of the twentieth century, whilst to the right of the locomotive can be seen the building which provided access from Union Road. (Commercial postcard / T.E. Atkins collection)

12. This photograph from the summer of 1937 gives us a closer view of the building and stairways serving the northern entrance. When opened in 1888 there were stairs to the up platform only, although a separate path from the end of the down platform led up to the road. The footbridge and down platform stairs were added in 1901. This office stocked tickets which showed the station of origin as 'Leyton (U.R.O.)' indicating that they had been issued by the Union Road Office. A change of street name resulted in it becoming known as the Langthorne Road entrance in 1949 and from 8th April 1958 its hours of opening were reduced. (British Rail)

13. Class N7 0-6-2T No.9651 makes a wonderfully nostalgic sight as she pulls away from Leyton with a train for Liverpool Street in the final days of regular steam operated passenger services over the line. The station was little altered in connection with the LPTB takeover, although the main street level building received a new frontage. (RAS Marketing)

14. This southward view from the 1960s shows a London Transport Central Line train that has just passed Leyton signal box and is about to descend into the tunnel. This box, which was sited on the opposite side of the road bridge from the station, dated from November 1899, and had a thirty-one lever Dutton Trigger frame. It was subsequently set back a few feet and modified in connection with the Underground extension. In this form it was inspected on behalf of the Ministry of Transport in May 1947 and it remained in use until 4th November 1971. The original route from Stratford can be seen to the right of the train, along with part of the goods and coal yard, which officially closed from 6th May 1968. (G. Pember)

15. Although the premises were extensively rebuilt in the late 1880s, the original 1856 station house, which adjoined an exit leading from the down platform survived much longer. Its end was hastened by the construction of the M11 Link Road however and it was demolished in May 1996. This photograph was taken ten years earlier. (A.D. Simpson)

16. The same scheme also resulted in the complete closure of the Langthorne Road entrance from 3rd March 1995. The building was demolished during early July 1996 and the adjoining brick arch bridge was removed a month later on 18th August. (J.E. Connor)

17.   Despite the changes that have taken place over the years, the former Great Eastern Railway station at Leyton still retains many of its pre-grouping architectural features, although it is now fitted with refinements such as CCTV security cameras. This photograph was taken in the spring of 2007 and shows a train of London Underground 1992 stock arriving at the eastbound platform.   (G.W. Goslin)

The LPTB published a series of leaflets in connection with the various Central Line extensions which took place in the late 1940s. This one, produced in 1947, featured a bow and arrow design, with three dots to symbolise the stations at Stratford, Leyton and Leytonstone.

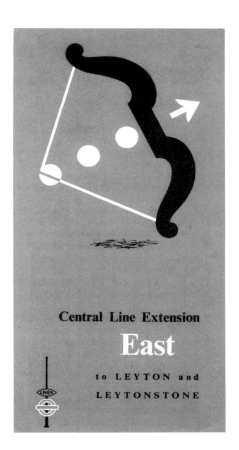

Central Line Extension

**East**

to LEYTON and
LEYTONSTONE

24. The routes linking Stratford with Epping and Hainault via Newbury Park were operated from the late 1940s until the end of 1962 by trains of Standard tube stock. This view shows the rear of one of these units standing beside the eastbound platform at Leytonstone. (Lens of Sutton collection)

25. When rebuilding was complete, the up side, designated 'westbound' by London Transport, had two platform faces, whilst the eastbound retained one. This photograph, dating from the 1990s, looks towards Stratford and shows the rear of a train departing for central London. (J.L. Crook)

26. The rebuilt station was provided with a sub-surface ticket hall, accessed by subways from both sides of the line. This view, taken in 2007, shows the entrance from Church Lane, which retains much of its late 1940s styling. In recent times, the subway has featured a number of mosaic panels, commissioned in 2000 and designed by the artist Steve Lobb, which depict scenes from films made by the famous director Alfred Hitchcock. Hitchcock, who was born about a half-mile from the station in 1899, started his career in the 1920s with British films such as *The Lodger* starring Ivor Novello and June, but later moved to America where he died in 1980. (J.E.

# SNARESBROOK

Another one of the original stations on the line, Snaresbrook was shown in GER working timetables as being 3miles 4chains from Stratford and is seen here as it appeared on the Ordnance Survey map of 1919, with a goods yard, dating from around 1870, to the left of the passenger platforms. The station underwent extensive alterations in 1893, when a bay was added to the down side for *"Short Trains to and from London"*, and five years later, in November 1898, it was renamed 'Snaresbrook & Wanstead'. In 1903 an additional entrance for ticket holders was provided on the up side, with stairs leading from the High Street below. Before this, access was by way of the original 1856 station house which faced onto the down platform. The station's name was amended to 'Snaresbrook for Wanstead' in 1929 and remained as such until 14th December 1947, when, on the opening of Wanstead on the new Leytonstone - Newbury Park Underground link, it reverted to the original title of plain 'Snaresbrook'.

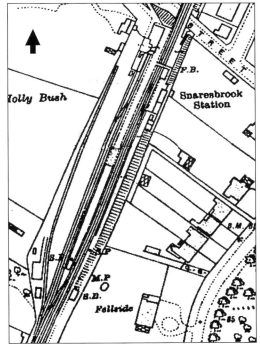

27. Here we see the 1903 up side entrance soon after opening, with a member of staff at the top of the stairs waiting to check tickets. The original ECR station house is visible to the top left and has been fitted with an awning dating from 1883. In October 1910 it was stated that an additional exit was to be provided on the down side and that the local council was willing to pay half the cost. (Commercial postcard/T.E. Atkins collection)

28. Still in the early years of the twentieth century we stand on the down platform and see a train approaching. The GER Way & Works Committee minutes of 30th July 1878 mentioned that a contract was to be awarded for a footbridge at the station and presumably this is the one featured here. In December 1914 it was reported that the up platform needed to be widened from 11ft to 15ft and the awning extended so that it matched its counterpart on the down side. (Commercial postcard / P. Laming collection)

29. This view looks north in the 1930s and includes the goods yard together with the 1893 bay platform to the left. The signal box replaced a cabin of 1876 when the station layout was altered in 1893 and contained a thirty-two lever Saxby & Farmer frame. From 21st September 1947 only five levers remained in use and the box was completely closed shortly before electric services were extended from Leytonstone to Woodford on 14th December 1947. The goods yard, which was latterly worked from a ground frame, closed on and from 1st August 1949. (A.D. Simpson collection)

30.   Looking north in the late 1960s we can see that the station still retained much of its GER character, including the distinctive style of valancing, although the footbridge had a replacement span. Also apparent are the differing awning heights on the up side, where the earlier canopy at the far end meets the extension put up in 1915.   (J.E. Connor)

31.   This photograph shows the trackbed of the former bay platform line, which was purely a goods siding after 1947 and was abandoned in 1950 after closure to goods.

32. Snaresbrook has retained its 1856 station house, although the entrance was modified by London Transport in October 1948, when an additional booking hall was also provided on the westbound side. Here we see the frontage of the original building as it appeared in May 1986. (A.D. Simpson)

33. Between the stations at Snaresbrook and what is now South Woodford, lay a level crossing and goods yard at Eagle Lane. This undated view includes the signal box, which opened in 1899 and had an eighteen lever McKenzie & Holland frame, along with a wheel to operate the crossing gates. The level crossing was closed from 30th November 1947 and the box was abolished soon after. The goods yard, which, like the box was located north of the crossing, dated from 15th May 1899 and officially remained in use until 18th April 1966. (A.D. Simpson collection)

LONDON, STRATFORD, WOODFORD, LOUGHTON, EPPING, and ONGAR.—Gt. East. & Nth. London. **Sundays.**

June 1869

# SOUTH WOODFORD

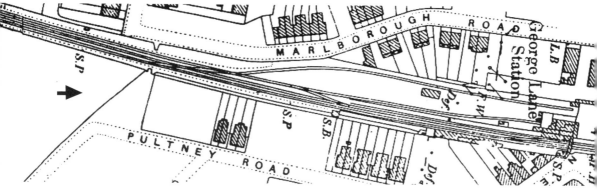

The station, which is shown on this Ordnance Survey map of 1897, opened as George Lane on 22nd August 1856 and was located 3miles 69chains from Stratford by way of the original route. It comprised two platforms and was entered through the main station building-cum-house, which stood on the down side, south of the level crossing. Behind the platforms, to the west, lay the goods yard, comprising two sidings, which dated from 1880 and continued to serve its intended purpose until closing on 6th January 1964.

34.   This rare view shows the station whilst its original building of 1856 was still in use. The footbridge on the left dated from 1880 and, according to the Way & Works Committee minutes, was designed with *separate ways for passengers and other users*. Originally it was open to the elements, but a roof was added in 1891. (W.L.F. Wastell/A.D. Simpson collection)

35. This delightful view looks north and shows the station as it appeared around 1910, with the goods yard evident behind the down platform on the left. Is the demure young lady reading a book or checking the times of her next train into town? (Commercial postcard / T.E. Atkins collection)

36. In 1910 the old station house was demolished and replaced by a new building which is seen here. As with other locations along this stretch of line, the level crossing was closed from 30th November 1947. (Commercial postcard / T.E. Atkins collection)

37.  Photographs of larger tender locomotives working the line seem to be very rare, so although of indifferent quality, this view just had to be included. It shows one of H.N. Gresley's Class K2 2-6-0s heading south with a freight train sometime in the 1930s. The station was renamed South Woodford (George Lane) on 5th July 1937. The running-in board partly visible on the left, displays 'George Lane For South Woodford' but it appears that only the final section of the title is picked out in white. Could the photograph have been taken just after renaming?  (Stations UK)

38.  This view again looks north and includes the signal box, which although dating from 1880, had to be moved a little further south in 1905-6 when the up platform was extended. The box was recorded as having a Stevens Tappet frame with nineteen levers in 1891, but by the summer of 1899, the number of levers had increased to twenty-three. It remained in use until 12th October 1947 when it was replaced by a brick cabin of LPTB design.  (Stations UK)

39. Here we see a westbound Central Line train formed of Standard tube stock, departing from South Woodford on 7th July 1957. The 1947 signal cabin, which stands on the right, was equipped with twenty-three mechanical and thirty-five power levers. It ceased to be a signal box in 1972, but was retained as a relay room and still serves as such under the present replacement signalling. The goods yard closed from 6th January 1964, but, apart from an additional up side ticket office provided in March 1948, the passenger station remained little changed under LT ownership. The bracketed suffix 'George Lane' was officially dropped from the station's name from 14th December 1947, but surprisingly continued to be displayed on some of the platform roundels in 2007. (P.J. Kelley)

# WOODFORD

Opened with the line to Loughton on 22nd August 1856, Woodford was located 4miles 77chains from Stratford by way of the original route. It comprised two platforms from the outset and, in common with all the other intermediate stations apart from Leytonstone, it had its main building on the down side. Both platforms were south of the level crossing but the up platform was fully 'staggered' to the south of that serving the down. This situation was changed when both platforms were extended in the 1870s. Originally the premises were oil-lit after dark, but gas lighting seems to have been installed in 1874, as the Way & Works Committee minutes refer to the fitting of 'Wavish' lamps. More changes came during the next decade, with the erection of a footbridge in 1887 and general down side improvements, including a new platform canopy. Towards the end of 1889 it was agreed to build a temporary line from the east side of the branch, which would stretch to a distance of around 1 mile and allow contractors to transport building materials to the Claybury Asylum which was then under construction. In 1892 there were major up side improvements in the shape of a new booking hall and a lengthy platform canopy. Finally, in the summer of 1914 the up platform was extended and widened on its eastern side to provide a bay, whilst five carriage sidings were added alongside. A single siding for coal traffic was authorised in February 1864 and the yard, which was enlarged in 1874, remained in use until 18th April 1966. The Ordnance Survey map shows the station layout as it was in 1920.

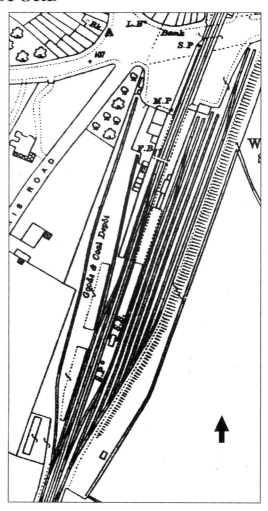

45. This view looks north at an unknown date, possibly in the 1920s, and includes the original down platform and part of the coal yard on the left. This opened prior to 1872 and was closed from 6th January 1964. The signal box dated from 1876 and was the last survivor of the hipped roof boxes built in that year by Saxby & Farmer at all six stations, Leyton to Buckhurst Hill. The reason for its longevity was that the track layout at Buckhurst Hill never changed after 1876. It closed on 20th November 1948. (A.D. Simpson collection)

46. This is W.N. Ashbee's attractive street level building, which was provided for the rebuilt station of 1892 and is seen here when fairly new. It was still in use in 2007, although various modifications have taken place over the years, including the loss of the distinctive entrance canopy. (Commercial postcard / A.D. Simpson collection)

47. Railway staff seemed to enjoy posing for photographers in the early part of the twentieth century! This undated view looks north and shows the replacement down platform on the left, with the street level building and its attendant stairway rising up above the canopy. On the right is the canopy on the 1881 up platform waiting rooms block, which was retained in the rebuilding. London Transport made very little in the way of alterations, although an additional peak-period booking office was opened at the south end in 1948. (Commercial postcard / T.E. Atkins collection)

48. The old station house of 1856 appeared to be in good shape when recorded in the 1990s. This view was taken from the south end of the up platform and shows a Central Line train formed of 1962 stock heading towards Epping. The wall in the foreground marks the site of the former level crossing, which closed in 1948. (G.W. Goslin)

# LOUGHTON

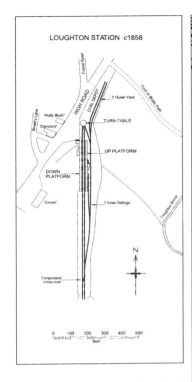

LOUGHTON STATION c1858

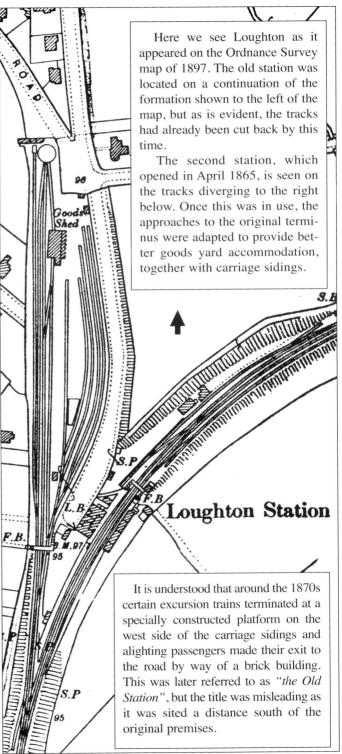

Here we see Loughton as it appeared on the Ordnance Survey map of 1897. The old station was located on a continuation of the formation shown to the left of the map, but as is evident, the tracks had already been cut back by this time.

The second station, which opened in April 1865, is seen on the tracks diverging to the right below. Once this was in use, the approaches to the original terminus were adapted to provide better goods yard accommodation, together with carriage sidings.

Loughton Station

It is understood that around the 1870s certain excursion trains terminated at a specially constructed platform on the west side of the carriage sidings and alighting passengers made their exit to the road by way of a brick building. This was later referred to as *"the Old Station"*, but the title was misleading as it was sited a distance south of the original premises.

The map above shows the original 1856 terminus at Loughton, which stood to the east of the High Road, by the future site of Lopping Hall. The old station comprised two platforms and had its principal building on the down side. Although no photographs of it are known, it is thought to have been of the single storey type and probably built largely of wood. At the northern end was the booking hall, which also handled parcels and was adapted to accommodate a telegraph office in 1858. Apart from the two platform roads, which terminated at a small turntable, there was also a loop on the east side. This was again linked to the turntable but also led to a double tracked coal depot which lay a little to the north of the passenger station.

49. This photograph was taken from the public footbridge spanning the tracks leading to the goods yard and carriage sidings which can be seen towards the bottom of the map reproduced on the previous page. It shows some of the sidings in the foreground and the 1865 station entrance to the right. Loughton became a popular destination for visitors to Epping Forest and the carriage sidings were subsequently enlarged to accommodate stock from excursion trains. From the 1890s, special trains conveying school children from inner east London would arrive at Loughton, where the youngsters would be led along the road to enjoy a few hours of fresh air at the Shaftesbury Retreat. Although under the watchful eye of the teachers, they were deemed unruly by some of the residents and the perceived antagonism resulted in some children referring to their destination as *"Lousy Loughton"*, a decidedly undeserved epithet which continued to be used among young East Enders at least into the 1930s. To the left of the station building stands a cabmen's shelter dating from 1889, whilst behind that is a loading dock of around 1865 and some stables added in 1890. The signal box visible in the distance was known as Loughton 'B' and dated from 1886. Its Saxby & Farmer frame originally contained twenty-five levers, but the number was later increased to thirty-one. By 1893 it had been renamed 'Loughton Yard' and it remained in use until 26th February 1933. Loughton 'A' box, subsequently renamed 'Loughton Junction' was located to the south of the station and also dated from 1886. This was fitted with a Saxby & Farmer Gridiron frame and originally housed thirty levers. The number increased to thirty-one by 1921 and then to fifty when 'Loughton Yard' closed in 1933. From then on, Loughton Junction box became known simply as Loughton. It survived into the postwar era, but was finally abolished on 25th September 1948 and replaced by a new LT cabin the following day. Loughton goods yard closed from 18th April 1966. (Commercial postcard / T.E. Atkins collection)

50. This view looks towards Ongar and was taken from the London end of the up platform on 3rd April 1937. To the left we see part of the footbridge which spanned the approach to the sidings, whilst in the centre is the main station building. Apart from this, the original accommodation was fairly sparse, although the premises developed over the years. It seems that the platforms were extended around 1875 and five years later a passenger footbridge was added. This was located towards the country end, but is hidden in this view by the up side canopy. In September 1882 it was decided to raise the height of the down platform from 2ft to 3ft, then, in 1896, the up platform was widened and provided with new buildings. These were fitted with awnings from the outset, but the down platform had to wait until 1905-6, when it was eventually provided with the canopy which is visible here. (H.C. Casserley)

**LONDON, STRATFORD, WOODFORD, LOUGHTON, EPPING, and ONGAR.**—Great Eastern.

| Miles | Down. | Week Days—*Continued below.* | | | | | | | | | | | | | | | | | | | | | | |
|---|---|---|---|---|---|---|---|---|---|---|---|---|---|---|---|---|---|---|---|---|---|---|---|---|
| | | mrn | mrn | mrn | a | b | a | b | b | b | b | a | a | a | b | a | b | a | b | a | b | a | b | a |
| | **Fenchurch St.**dep. | .... | 6 20 | 6 43 | 6 43 | 7 39 | .... | 8 7 | 8 18 | 8 35 | 8 50 | .... | 9 22 | .... | 9 51 | .... | 1012 | .... | 1047 | .... | 1116 | .... | 1227 | .... |
| 1½ | Stepney | .... | 6 27 | 6 50 | 6 50 | 7 45 | .... | 8 12 | 8 25 | 8 41 | 8 56 | .... | 9 29 | .... | 9 57 | .... | 1018 | .... | 1053 | .... | 1122 | .... | 1232 | .... |
| 2¼ | Burdett Road | .... | 6 29 | 6 52 | 6 52 | 7 47 | .... | 8 15 | 8 28 | 8 43 | 8 58 | .... | 9 31 | .... | 9 59 | .... | 1020 | .... | 1055 | .... | 1124 | .... | 1234 | .... |
| 3 | Bow Road | .... | 6 32 | 6 55 | 6 55 | 7 50 | .... | 8 18 | 8 34 | 8 46 | 9 1 | .... | 9 34 | .... | 10 2 | .... | 1023 | .... | 1058 | .... | 1127 | .... | 1238 | .... |
| — | **Liverpool St.** dp | 5 25 | 6 33 | 6 52 | 7 4 | 7 15 | 7 55 | .... | 8 28 | .... | 8 43 | 9 14 | 9 33 | 9 40 | .... | 10 0 | .... | 1030 | .... | 1111 | .... | 11 45 | 1222 | 1246 |
| — | **Bishopsgate** | 5 27 | 6 35 | 6 54 | 7 6 | .... | 7 57 | .... | .... | .... | 8 45 | .... | 9 35 | .... | .... | 10 2 | .... | .... | .... | 1113 | .... | 11 47 | 1225 | 1248 |
| — | Bethnal Green | 5 30 | 6 38 | 6 57 | 7 9 | .... | 8 0 | .... | 8 32 | .... | 8 48 | .... | 9 38 | .... | .... | 10 5 | .... | 1034 | .... | 1116 | .... | 11 50 | 1229 | 1251 |
| — | Globe Road * | 5 32 | 6 40 | 6 59 | 7 11 | .... | .... | .... | 8 34 | .... | 8 50 | .... | 9 40 | .... | .... | 10 7 | .... | .... | .... | 1118 | .... | 11 52 | 1231 | 1253 |
| — | Coborn Road † | 5 35 | 6 44 | 7 2 | 7 14 | .... | 8 4 | .... | 8 37 | .... | 8 53 | .... | 9 43 | .... | .... | 1010 | .... | 1039 | .... | 1121 | .... | 11 55 | 1234 | 1256 |
| 4½ | **Stratford** ‡ | 6 3 | 7 0 | 7 10 | 7 20 | 7 56 | 8 9 | 8 26 | 8 44 | 8 55 | 9 7 | 9 26 | 9 48 | 9 52 | 10 8 | 1016 | 1031 | .... | 11 3 | 1126 | 1133 | 12 3 | 1245 | 1 1 |
| 5½ | Leyton | 6 7 | 7 4 | 7 13 | 7 24 | 8 0 | 8 12 | 8 30 | 8 48 | 8 59 | 9 11 | .... | 9 51 | 9 56 | 1012 | 1019 | .... | .... | 11 7 | 1129 | 1137 | 12 8 | 1249 | 1 4 |
| 6¼ | Leytonstone | 6 11 | 7 8 | 7 17 | 7 28 | 8 4 | 8 16 | 8 34 | 8 52 | 9 3 | 9 15 | .... | 9 55 | 10 0 | 1016 | 1023 | .... | 1049 | 1111 | 1133 | 1142 | 12 13 | 1253 | 1 8 |
| 7½ | Snaresbrook § | 6 15 | 7 11 | 7 21 | 7 32 | 8 8 | 8 19 | 8 38 | 8 56 | 9 7 | 9 19 | 9 35 | 9 59 | 10 4 | 1020 | 1027 | .... | 1053 | 1114 | 1137 | 1146 | 12 17 | 1257 | 1 11 |
| 8¼ | George Lane ‖ | 6 18 | 7 14 | 7 24 | 7 35 | 8 11 | 8 22 | 8 41 | 8 59 | 9 10 | 9 22 | .... | 10 2 | 10 7 | 1023 | 1030 | .... | 1056 | .... | 1140 | 1149 | 12 20 | 1 0 | 1 14 |
| 9½ | **Woodford** ¶ 281 | 6 22 | 7 18 | 7 28 | 7 39 | 8 15 | 8 26 | 8 45 | 9 3 | 9 14 | 9 26 | 9 40 | 10 6 | 1011 | 1027 | 1034 | 1041 | 11 0 | .... | 1144 | 1153 | 12 24 | 1 4 | 1 18 |
| 10¾ | Buckhurst Hill | 6 26 | 7 22 | | 7 43 | 8 20 | | 8 49 | | 9 18 | 9 30 | 9 44 | 1010 | 1016 | 1031 | | 1045 | 11 4 | .... | | 1157 | 12 28 | 1 8 | |
| 12 | **Loughton** | 6 30 | 7 25 | | 7 55 | 8 24 | | 8 55 | | 9 22 | 9 33 | 9 49 | 1013 | | 1034 | | 1051 | 1110 | .... | | 12 3 | 12 31 | 1 15 | |
| 13½ | Chigwell Lane | .... | .... | To Ilford. | 7 59 | .... | To Ilford. | 8 59 | To Ilford. | .... | .... | 9 53 | .... | To Ilford. | .... | To Ilford. | 1055 | 1114 | .... | To Ilford. | 12 7 | 12c36 | 1 19 | To Ilford. |
| 15½ | Theydon Bois | .... | .... | | 8 4 | .... | | 9 3 | | .... | .... | 9 58 | .... | | .... | | 11 0 | 1118 | .... | | 1211 | 12c40 | 1 24 | |
| 17 | **Epping** | .... | .... | | 8 12 | .... | | 9 12 | | .... | .... | 10 5 | .... | | .... | | 11 7 | 1122 | .... | | 1216 | 12c44 | 1 31 | |
| 19½ | North Weald | .... | .... | | 8 17 | .... | | 9 17 | | .... | .... | .... | .... | | .... | | 1112 | .... | .... | | .... | .... | 1 37 | |
| 21½ | Blake Hall | .... | .... | | 8 22 | .... | | 9 21 | | .... | .... | .... | .... | | .... | | 1116 | .... | .... | | .... | .... | 1 43 | |
| 23¼ | **Ongar** arr. | .... | .... | | 8 27 | .... | | 9 25 | | .... | .... | 1016 | .... | | .... | | 1120 | .... | .... | | 1227 | .... | 1 47 | |

July 1903

51. As part of the electrification scheme, a new station with two island platforms and three tracks was erected around 200-300yds north-east of the premises of 1865. It was designed for the LNER by the architect John Murray Easton and was brought into use on 28th April 1940, although passengers had to wait until 21st November 1948 before electric services were extended from Woodford. In the meantime steam locomotives continued to haul the trains as seen in this photograph, which looks towards Epping. After the station opened, its predecessor disappeared although the date of its actual demolition has not been verified. (Lens of Sutton collection)

52. The station of 1940 has remained substantially unaltered into the twenty-first century and since May 1994 has been a Grade II listed structure. This view was taken in the 1990s and looks towards London. (G.W. Goslin)

# DEBDEN

Located 8miles 65chains from Stratford by way of Loughton Branch Junction, this station opened with the extension to Ongar on 24th April 1865. It was originally named Chigwell Road, but became Chigwell Lane after just a few months, on 1st December 1865.

At first there was only one platform, but another was added when the section between Loughton and Epping was doubled in late 1892. Traffic remained light however and Chigwell Lane was closed in the interests of wartime economy from 22nd May 1916 until 3rd February 1919.

The map below shows the layout of the station, as it appeared soon after the route was doubled. The goods yard lay to the north of the passenger platforms and remained in use for just over a century, from 1865 until 18th April 1966.

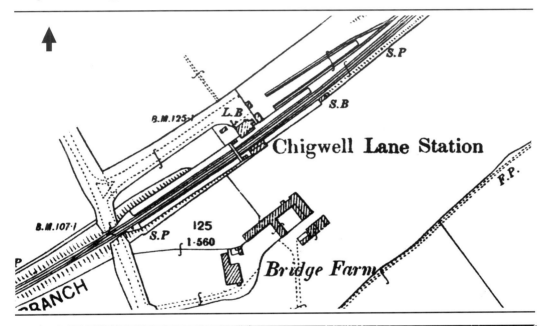

LONDON, STRATFORD, WOODFORD, LOUGHTON, EPPING, and ONGAR.—Great Eastern.

*(Timetable, June 1920. Down services — Week Days and Sundays — for stations including Liverpool Street, Fenchurch Street, Stratford, Leyton, Leytonstone, Snaresbrook, George Lane, Woodford, Buckhurst Hill, Loughton, Chigwell Lane, Theydon Bois, Epping, North Weald, Blake Hall, and Ongar.)*

53. This photograph looks towards Loughton and includes the signal box which dated from 1887. This accommodated a twenty-two lever Saxby & Farmer Rocker frame and remained in use until 25th June 1949. Near the centre of the view we see the up side building of 1892, whilst to the right stands the original 1865 house. Because Chigwell Lane station retained oil lighting for many years it was sometimes referred to by staff as *'Paraffin Junction'*.   (Lens of Sutton collection)

54.  The advent of a nearby housing development, built by the London County Council and named 'Debden', resulted in the station adopting this title from 25th September 1949. It is known that 'Chigwell Lane' appeared on temporary LT roundel type signs, but no photographs showing these have been located. On the date of renaming, tube services were extended from Loughton to Epping, so the sight of steam-hauled passenger trains over the section became a rarity. This photograph, taken on 28th April 1962, shows Class J15 0-6-0 No 65476 passing through with the Locomotive Club of Great Britain *'Great Eastern Suburban Railtour'* bound for Ongar.  (B.P. Pask)

# EPPING

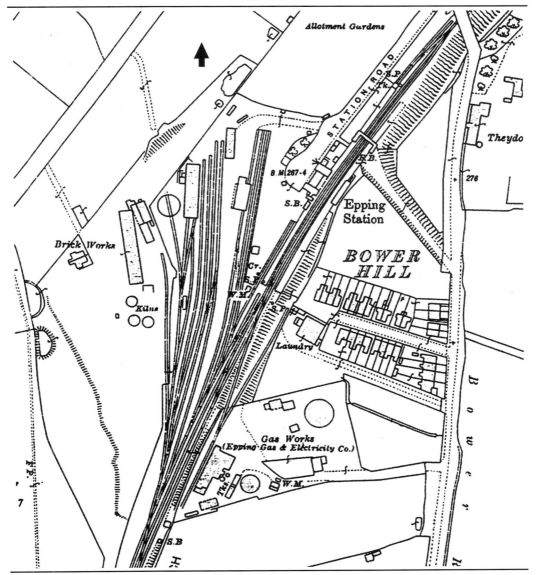

Epping station, which was located 12miles 36chains from Stratford by way of the original route, is shown on this Ordnance Survey map of 1920. It was a passing place from the outset. The two platforms were originally slightly staggered, but in 1880 the up platform was shortened at the south end and lengthened to the north, bringing them into line. Then in connection with the 1892 widening from Loughton, both platforms were extended southwards, increasing their length from 340ft to 520ft. In addition to the station, the map also shows the goods yard and locomotive depot, which were both sited west of the running lines. The goods yard was increased to the size shown here in 1893, having previously comprised just four roads. On the opposite side of the line can be seen a siding serving the gasworks, whilst below this is a twelve-lever ground frame, also dating from 1893, which controlled connections to and from the yard.

61. We start our look at Epping with this pre-grouping view taken from a commercial postcard printed in the early twentieth century. It was taken from the down platform and shows passengers preparing to board a train which is arriving at the up side. The signal box on the left dated from 1887 and was equipped with a twenty-three lever Saxby & Farmer frame. Behind this stands the 1865 station house and the footbridge which was erected in 1891-2. No platform canopies were ever provided here. (T.E. Atkins collection)

62. A class N7 0-6-2T appears to be receiving attention from a member of her crew as she waits to depart with a train for Liverpool Street in the 1930s. In the background we see the footbridge, which by this time had lost its roof. The picture seems to have been taken from the up platform starting signal, so we can only assume that the photographer had permission! (T.E. Atkins collection)

63. We leave the platforms briefly to view the station exterior as it appeared in April 1938. At first glance the 1865 building looks little altered, but on closer inspection we can see that the full length awning above the entrance had been shortened so that it only covered the doorway. Another change can be noted to the left, where the living accommodation had been extended in 1891, presumably to house the stationmaster's growing family. (British Rail)

64. From September 1949 until November 1957, passengers for stations beyond Epping had to alight from their tube train and cross the footbridge to join the steam-worked push-pull service. This view shows a train of flat-ended 1935 stock on the left and ex-GER Class F5 2-4-2T No.67202 on the right. Comparison with photograph No.62 shows that a water crane had been positioned closer to the up platform building to serve the needs of the short push-pull trains. (Lens of Sutton collection)

65. Although a small number of locomotives had previously been stabled at Epping, there was initially no depot as such. The situation changed in the early 1890s however, when the company decided to provide a shed and associated sidings. The contract for construction was duly let and work commenced in 1893. The shed itself could accommodate six tank engines and is seen here in rather poor condition on 14th July 1947. The locomotive just visible on the extreme left is standing on the road which led to a 50ft turntable, necessary for servicing the tender locomotives sometimes used on branch freights. (A.F. Cook)

66. The shed was partially rebuilt with a new roof in the postwar years and provided with a steel-framed coaling shelter, as seen in this view which was taken on 29th April 1956. Although the majority of locomotives employed on the Epping-Ongar push-pull trains were ex-GER 2-4-2Ts, other types were tried, including 0-4-4Ts and an ex-GNR Class C12 4-4-2T. Once the line to Ongar had been electrified the depot became surplus to requirements and was therefore closed. (H.C. Casserley)

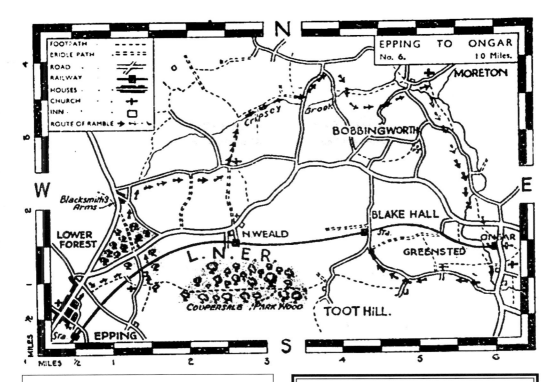

FOOTPATH . - - - - -
BRIDLE PATH . = = = =
ROAD .
RAILWAY
HOUSES .
CHURCH . +
INN . □
ROUTE OF RAMBLE →

EPPING TO ONGAR
No. 6.          10 Miles.

N

W          E

S

MORETON

BOBBINGWORTH

Cripsey Brook

Blacksmith's Arms

LOWER FOREST

N WEALD

L.N.E.R.

BLAKE HALL

GREENSTED

ONGAR

COOPERSALE PARK WOOD

TOOT HILL.

Sta.

EPPING

MILES ½    1    2    3    4    5    6

## ROUTE OF RAMBLE No. 6

### EPPING TO ONGAR

### 10 MILES

Take cheap day ticket from Liverpool Street L·N·E·R Station to Epping, 2/3, 3rd class return. Weekdays by any train at or after 9 a.m. Sundays by any train. Excess fare from Ongar, 9d.

Go forward from the station to the road, turn left up to the town and go right through it to the Abridge road, there turning right to the Coopersale path on the left. Follow this to the village, turn left under the railway to the Lower Forest, keeping on through it and, right of the Blacksmiths' Arms at Woodside, join the North Weald road, where, right, go on to a path, left, just before the church. (4 miles). Follow this path up to a brick bridge, here go right parallel to the brook to a lane and take the forward green continuation, where turn left up to the signpost and there go right, bearing right down to the brook and a forward path close to it which leads to Moreton village. (7 miles). Go through the village to the church, take, right, the opposite path (swing gate), re-cross the brook and continue to the road, turning left to the brook once more, where either follow the path or the road on map to Ongar station. (10 miles).

If time allows go down the High Street to a wide path on the right by the Institute and take it to Greensted church. From this you can rejoin the railway at Blake Hall or retrace the route to Ongar station. The extra fare is 9d. There is a more direct alternative footpath route from Coopersale by Ongar Park Wood, Toot Hill, and Greensted to Ongar, (see map).

# FARM COLLECTION

### AND

# DELIVERY SERVICE

#### FROM

### ONGAR

### BLAKE HALL

### NORTH WEALD

Commencing MONDAY, 15th OCTOBER, 1928, the Company will be prepared to deliver Loads of Agricultural Traffic to farms from the stations shewn above.

Collection of such Traffic for forwarding by rail will also be undertaken.

The charges for the service will be:

Up to 1 mile - - - - 2/- per ton
Over 1 and up to 3 miles - - 3/- ,,

Over 3 miles—6d. per mile for each additional mile.

Minimum charge as for 20 cwts.

Special charges will be made for the cartage of Hay and Straw.

Further information as to the service can be obtained from the Station Master at the Stations named, or the District Goods Manager, L.N.E.R., York Road, King's Cross, London, N.

London, October, 1928.

LNER

A.D. Simpson collection                    K. Romig collection

75. This fine 'official' view shows the station exterior in 1938, with gates providing road access to the goods yard on the left. In the distance we also see the signal box of 1888, the locomotive water tank which dated from opening and, partially hidden, the engine shed. (British Rail)

76. Having entered the station, we look west along the platform to view the single-road locomotive shed which was erected in 1865. In the foreground stands Class F5 2-4-2T No.7147, carrying an Ongar destination board, whilst a similar engine lurks in the gloom of the shed building. The photograph was taken on 11th June 1938 and also includes part of the coaling stage behind the wagon to the right of No.7147. The shed seems to have been demolished in the 1940s, although the siding and engine pit are thought to have survived into the latter days of steam operation. (H.C. Casserley)

77. This view was taken on 11th October 1952 from a train which was either leaving or arriving at the terminus. To the left we see the signal box which, as already stated, was built in 1888. This was originally fitted with a twenty-lever Saxby & Farmer Duplex frame, but a new frame containing thirty levers was provided in 1949. To our right lies the goods yard. The sidings seen here date largely from 1865. Another siding, to the south of the goods shed (see map), was added when the facilities were slightly enlarged in 1900. (B.A. Crouch / GERS collection)

78. We now move in a little closer on the same day to get a better view of the goods shed and its attendant crane, which had a capacity of two tons. Freight traffic ceased to be handled at Ongar on 18th April 1966 and the yard was subsequently abandoned. (B.A. Crouch / GERS collection)

79. Continuing into the early days of electrification, we see a train of 1935 tube stock which has arrived from Epping and is about to return. The signal box, which is visible in the background, was closed on 23rd March 1969 and later demolished. (Lens of Sutton collection)

80. Moving into the preservation era, we see a Class 117 DMU standing at the platform alongside a group of Finnish steam locomotives which are stored on a length of specially laid 5ft gauge track. In 2007 the Epping Ongar Railway operated up to six return DMU trips on Sundays and Bank Holidays between Ongar and Coopersale, west of North Weald, where the Society planned to erect a halt. (A.D. Simpson)

# RODING VALLEY

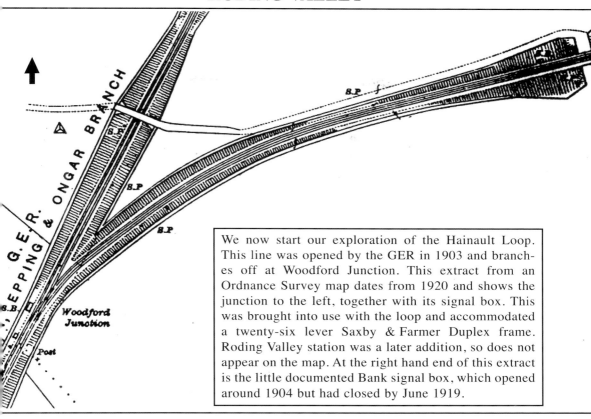

We now start our exploration of the Hainault Loop. This line was opened by the GER in 1903 and branches off at Woodford Junction. This extract from an Ordnance Survey map dates from 1920 and shows the junction to the left, together with its signal box. This was brought into use with the loop and accommodated a twenty-six lever Saxby & Farmer Duplex frame. Roding Valley station was a later addition, so does not appear on the map. At the right hand end of this extract is the little documented Bank signal box, which opened around 1904 but had closed by June 1919.

81. This 1911 view looks north-east towards the junction and includes the 1903 signal box on the left. Roding Valley was subsequently erected just east of where the Loop commences on the right. The Junction signal box was abolished on 7th August 1948, after which the junction points were controlled from the LT box at Woodford. (D. Brennand collection)

82. Roding Valley Halt was erected by the LNER just 69chains from Woodford and was opened on 3rd February 1936. It was financed by the building firm of W & C French Ltd, who were developing an estate of around 1,500 houses nearby, and comprised a pair of 500ft long platforms. This photograph looks towards Woodford Junction in the 1930s and includes the main building, which accommodated the booking office, on the right. This was constructed of brick, but the waiting shelter opposite was wooden. To the left of the shelter we can see a sign which advises passengers that this was the platform for trains to Woodford and London. (British Rail)

83. Although the station was shown as Roding Valley *Halt* on tickets and other LNER printed material, this view, which is thought to date from the late 1930s, includes a running-in board to the left which shows the name simply as 'Roding Valley'. The main building, which stood on the north side of the line, was accessed from Station Way and is just visible beyond the footbridge. (Lens of Sutton collection)

84. Here we see an ex-GER 2-4-2T bringing a Woodford bound train into Roding Valley Halt, sometime in the 1930s. (A.D. Simpson collection)

85. The station was rebuilt around 1949 and is seen here looking towards Woodford Junction at an unknown date, possibly in the 1960s. The line between Woodford and Hainault was the last section of the Loop to be electrified, with the new services commencing on 21st November 1948. (Lens of Sutton collection)

# CHIGWELL

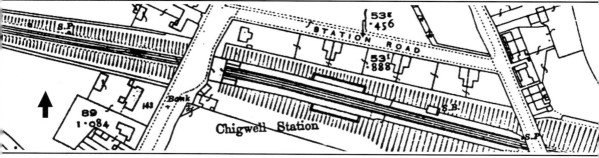

Located 2 miles 21 chains from Woodford, Chigwell opened with the Hainault Loop on 1st May 1903 and is shown on this Ordnance Survey map of 1919. The six semi-detached cottages lining the south side of Station Road were provided for the general staff, whilst the detached house at the west end accommodated the stationmaster. No goods yard was ever provided here.

86. The street level buildings at Chigwell, Grange Hill and Newbury Park were to the same design by W.N. Ashbee, Head of the Great Eastern Railway's Architectural Department. This view shows Chigwell, soon after completion, but prior to opening. The building has stood the test of time and, although subject to later alterations, remained in use in 2007. (Norfolk Railway Society)

87. Looking west in the 1930s, we have a good general view of the station and also see the signal box, which was fitted with a twenty-three lever Saxby & Farmer Duplex frame. The box dated from the line's opening and remained in use until 14th December 1947. The platforms here and at the other original Loop stations were 600ft. long excluding ramps. (Stations UK)

88. On 16th October 1940, the locomotive of the 5.34am train from Woodford to Ilford fell into a bomb crater near Chigwell and overturned. The stock was also derailed, but it is understood that there were no casualties. The incident resulted in both lines being blocked, but thanks to sterling work on behalf of the breakdown gang, services were restored by 5.35pm. This view records the clearing-up operations, but is also of interest as it shows some of the work which had already been done towards the electrification scheme. (British Rail)

89. When they were new, a number of 1967 Victoria Line trains were delivered to Hainault depot for testing, and were used on the shuttle service to Woodford. The units were fitted for Automatic Train Operation, and they maintained a presence on the route until May 1984. Here we see one of them departing from the Woodford-bound platform on 5th April 1968. At this time the awnings on both sides had been reduced in width at their western ends, but since then, similar rationalisation has taken place along their full length. (Pamlin Prints)

## Week Days—Continued below.

| | mrn | mrn | mrn | mrn | mrn | mrn | aft | aft | aft | aft | aft | aft | aft | aft | aft | aft | aft | aft | aft |
|---|---|---|---|---|---|---|---|---|---|---|---|---|---|---|---|---|---|---|---|
| Fenchurch Street dep. | 6 45 | 7 30 | 8 18 | 9 22 | 9 51 | 10 55 | 12 7 | 1 9 | 1 45 | 2 6 | 2 12 | 2 20 | 2 50 | 3 30 | 4 13 | 4 13 | 4 45 | | 5 13 |
| Liverpool Street.. " | 6 52 | 7 55 | 8 28 | 9 40 | 10 0 | 11 11 | 12 95 | | 1 20 | | 2 25 | 2 41 | 3 8 | 3 38 | | 4 22 | 4 38 | | 5 20 |
| Stratford (Wt.Ham) " | 7 10 | 8 | 9 8 | 4 49 | 9 52 | 10 16 | 11 26 | 1 | 1 35 | | 2 33 | 2 51 | 3 23 | | 3 48 | 4 5 | | | 5 35 |
| Woodford ......... " | 7 28 | 8 26 | 9 | 3 | 10 11 | 10 34 | 11 44 | 1 18 | 1 55 | 2 39 | 2 40 | | 2 58 | 1 3 | 3 42 | 4 11 | 4 53 | 4 55 | 5 20 | 5 50 |
| Chigwell ............. | 7 35 | 8 31 | 9 | 8 | 10 16 | 10 38 | 11 49 | 1 23 | | | 2 44 | | 3 18 | | 3 49 | 4 16 | 4 58 | 5 | | 5 55 |
| Grange Hill ......... | 7 35 | 8 33 | 9 | 10 | 10 18 | 10 41 | 11 51 | 1 25 | | | 2 47 | | 3 20 | | 3 51 | 4 18 | | | | 5 58 |
| Hainault............... | 7 38 | 8 36 | 9 | 13 | 10 21 | 10 44 | 11 54 | 1 28 | | | 8 | | 3 23 | | 3 54 | 4 21 | | | | 6 1 |
| Fairlop ............. | 7 44 | 8 42 | 9 | 17 | 10 34 | 10 73 | 12 2 | 1 39 | 2 17 | 2 53 | | | | | | 4 36 | | | | 6 6 |
| Barkingside ......... | 7 47 | 8 45 | 9 | 20 | 10 37 | 11 6 | 12 51 | 1 35 | 2 20 | 2 56 | | | | | | 4 36 | | | | 6 6 |
| Newbury Park ....... | 7 49 | 8 47 | 9 | 22 | 10 39 | 11 8 | 12 7 | 1 37 | 2 22 | 2 58 | | | | | 4 7 | 4 39 | | | | 6 8 |
| Ilford 260 ......arr. | 7 53 | 8 51 | 9 | 26 | 10 43 | 11 12 | 12 11 | 1 41 | | | | | | | 4 11 | 4 42 | | | | 6 12 |
| Stratford (Wt.Ham)" | ...... | ...... | 9 | 43 | 10 56 | 11 27 | 12 25 | 1 53 | 2 40 | | 3 16 | | | | | 4 23 | 4 57 | | | 6 14 |
| Fenchurch Street. " | ...... | ...... | 10 | 1 | 11 14 | 11 48 | 12 22 | 12 | | 3 4 | 3 48 | | | | 4 9 | 4 45 | 5 14 | 5 52 | 6 14 | |
| Liverpool Street.. " | 8 17 | 8 17 | 9 | 44 | 11 14 | 11 48 | 12 54 | 2 18 | 2 55 | 3 25 | 3 55 | | | | 4 11 | 4 55 | 5 53 | 5 56 | | 6 33 |

90. Although it is not of the highest technical quality, this rare view shows a train passing Chigwell Nursery Siding and its attendant eight-lever ground frame box. The photographer was standing on the public footbridge to the north-east of the present Hycliffe Gardens and was looking towards Chigwell station, with the single road siding on the right, accessed by means of a fenced cart track. It is not known when the siding fell into disuse although the nursery it served was sold around 1922. (A.D. Simpson collection)

91. Continuing eastwards on a rising gradient of 1 in 100, the line reaches what railwaymen once called the "Quarter Mile Tunnel", although its length is generally described as being 260yds. The difference in height between structures built to main line standards and tube stock is very apparent as we see a 1960 Stock car at the rear of a Hainault - Woodford train disappearing into the gloom during the 1980s. (A.D. Simpson)

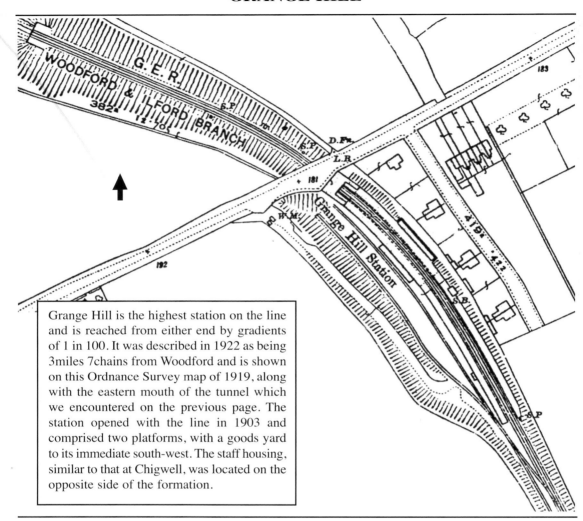

Grange Hill is the highest station on the line and is reached from either end by gradients of 1 in 100. It was described in 1922 as being 3 miles 7 chains from Woodford and is shown on this Ordnance Survey map of 1919, along with the eastern mouth of the tunnel which we encountered on the previous page. The station opened with the line in 1903 and comprised two platforms, with a goods yard to its immediate south-west. The staff housing, similar to that at Chigwell, was located on the opposite side of the formation.

**LONDON STRATFORD, ILFORD, CHIGWELL, WOODFORD, and LONDON.—Great Eastern.**

Week Days.

| Miles | | | | | | | | |
|---|---|---|---|---|---|---|---|---|
| | Liverpool Street ..dep. | | | | | | | |
| | Fenchurch Street ,, | | | | | | | |
| 4 | Stratford (Wt. Ham) ,, | | | | | | | |
| 7¼ | Ilford ................. ,, | | | | | | | |
| 9 | Newbury Park .......... ,, | | | | | | | |
| 9½ | Barkingside.......... ,, | | | | | | | |
| 10½ | Fairlop............. ,, | | | | | | | |
| 11½ | Grange Hill * ...... {arr. / dep. | | | | | | | |
| 12½ | Chigwell ........... ,, | | | | | | | |
| 14½ | Woodford 255 ...... arr. | | | | | | | |
| 24½ | Fenchurch Street ,, | | | | | | | |
| 23½ | Liverpool Street ... ,, | | | | | | | |

Week Days—*Continued.* / Sundays.

| | | | | | | | | | |
|---|---|---|---|---|---|---|---|---|---|
| Liverpool Street.......dep. | | | | | | | | | |
| Fenchurch Street...... ,, | | | | | | | | | |
| Stratford (West Ham) .. ,, | | | | | | | | | |
| Ilford................. ,, | | | | | | | | | |
| Newbury Park .......... ,, | | | | | | | | | |
| Barkingside............. ,, | | | | | | | | | |
| Fairlop................ ,, | | | | | | | | | |
| Grange Hill * .......... {arr. / dep | | | | | | | | | |
| Chigwell ........... arr. | | | | | | | | | |
| Woodford 255 ....... ,, | | | | | | | | | |
| Fenchurch Street ,, | | | | | | | | | |
| Liverpool Street....... ,, | | | | | | | | | |

June 1920

92. Despite their rural surroundings, the Hainault Loop stations were built in a style perhaps more suited to inner London. Here we see an ex-GER 2-4-2T passing beneath the street level building at Grange Hill and heading towards Hainault some time in the 1930s. (Stations UK)

93. This view, taken on 3rd April 1937, shows Class N7 0-6-2T No. 913 entering the station with the 11.11am train from Liverpool Street to Woodford. The 1903 signal box housed a twenty-four lever Saxby & Farmer Duplex frame and survived until 29th October 1948. (H.C. Casserley)

94. Around 5pm on 12th July 1944, a V1 'Doodlebug' fell in the goods yard causing serious damage to the station's northern end. The street level building was damaged beyond repair as can be seen from this photograph. Not surprisingly the train service was suspended and special buses were provided to convey passengers between Chigwell and Hainault. (British Rail)

95. Once the rubble had been cleared from the tracks it proved possible to reinstate the trains, although initially they had to pass through without stopping. This situation continued for a number of hours, but at 4.30pm on 13th July, less than twenty-four hours after the bomb struck, normal services were resumed. Here we see debris being piled onto a platform, as the station is prepared for reopening. The white paint on the canopy support columns, added to improve visibility in the blackout, was a familiar sight during World War II. (British Rail)

96. Looking north-west in the 1960s, we see both the passenger station and its adjoining two-road goods yard. This yard was opened in 1903 and closed from 4th October 1965. (Lens of Sutton collection)

97. The war damaged street level building at Grange Hill was demolished and replaced by the current entrance in 1949. This photograph was taken in 1987 and includes the former stationmaster's house which can be seen to the left. (A.D. Simpson)

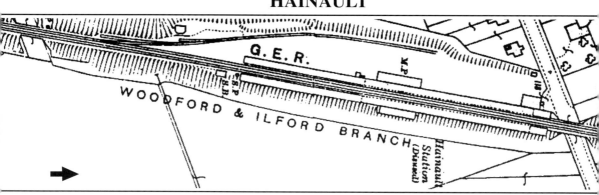

Hainault station is shown on this Ordnance Survey map of 1919, during the period that it was out of use. It opened with the line on 1st May 1903 and was provided with all the facilities required for dealing with heavy suburban traffic, but sadly it was little used. Still largely surrounded by open countryside and with no viable catchment area on the horizon, it was closed, along with the adjoining goods yard, from 1st October 1908. This was not to be the end however and the GER Way and Works Committee minutes of 4th May 1916 recorded that £116 was to be spent on *"station painting and repairs"*. It may have been that the company just wanted to keep the place in good order, or were there other intentions? During that year Henry Hughes & Son Ltd opened a factory nearby to produce navigational instruments and it has been suggested that the station might have seen a limited amount of use to serve the needs of the workforce.

98. Because it was closed in 1908, photographs of the station taken during the pre-grouping era are thought to be few and far between. This view shows it after completion, but before opening for traffic. We are looking north towards the well constructed red-brick buildings, but ominously there does not appear to be a house in sight. The tracks at this point were on embankment, but the platforms and buildings were supported on a succession of brick arches, of which the tops can be clearly seen to the left. (Norfolk Railway Society)

99. By the late 1920s it seems that part of the station was being used as residential accommodation, as passengers on passing trains often saw washing hanging on lines which had been tied between the platform lamp posts. By this time however, it seems that the Hughes' workforce was definitely using it when travelling to and from the factory, as the LNER working timetable of March 1927 made a reference to the validity of Hainault tickets. There was now more optimism about the area being developed, so from 3rd March 1930, it reopened to full public traffic, although the goods yard remained closed. The station had clearly weathered its wilderness years well, as can be seen from this photograph which was taken from the south end in June 1938. (H.C. Casserley)

100. For a while after reopening, the surrounding area still remained largely undeveloped and no building activity of note took place until 1940. This view shows the station entrance and exterior as it appeared in 1938, still surrounded by open spaces. (British Rail)

101. As part of the electrification scheme, work commenced on a depot for Underground stock on the west side of the line between Hainault and Grange Hill. Although virtually finished early in the war, it was not to serve its intended purpose until 1947. However, from June 1943 until January 1945 the depot was taken over by the 155 Railway Workshop Company of the Royal Engineers for the benefit of the US Army Transportation Corps and was used to assemble military railway vehicles for subsequent transportation to mainland Europe. (World War Two Railway Study Group)

102. After it became fully operational in 1948 the depot could be accessed from either end. Its facilities included a car shed, together with outdoor storage roads, a washing plant and a further shed used for carriage cleaning. This view looks north from the end of the station platforms and was taken in 1987. (A.D. Simpson)

103. The formation was widened at the station to accommodate five tracks, with the westernmost pair being part of the depot complex. From 31st May 1948 Central Line services to and from central London started and terminated at Hainault, so to increase capacity, the old Woodford-bound platform was rebuilt as an island. The work included the erection of new buildings, although the other platform was left more or less unaltered. This view shows a train of 1962 Stock waiting to depart for Ealing Broadway on 12th April 1968. (P.J. Kelley)

104. The alterations necessitated the construction of a new entrance, which is shown in this view taken from the opposite side of New North Road in 1987. (A.D. Simpson)

# FAIRLOP

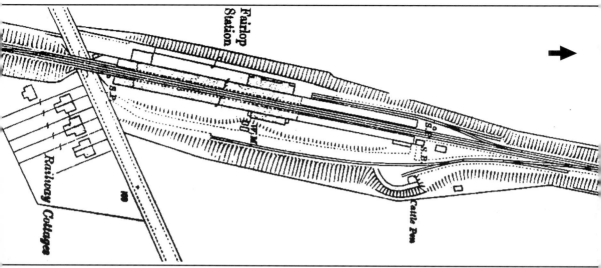

In steam days, trains travelling from the City by way of the Loop would either carry 'Fairlop via Woodford' or 'Fairlop via Ilford' destination boards. It was therefore regarded as an intermediate terminus, although in reality, services simply paused for several minutes then continued on their way. This Ordnance Survey map dates from 1919 and shows the station, which was 4miles 20chains from Woodford, along with its nearby staff housing. Apart from these there was little in the way of local development at the time, although it was the nearest station to the large Claybury Asylum. As can be seen, there were sidings on both sides of the line, although the goods depot is understood to have only occupied those to the east, so there is doubt regarding the intended use of the other, which survived at least until the 1930s.

105. This is the station entrance as it appeared around the time of opening in 1903, with members of staff standing by the doorway. As can be seen, the buildings here were of the same design as at Hainault. During World War I Fairlop was used by airmen travelling to and from the nearby Royal Naval Air Service field and the Royal Flying Corps base at Hainault Farm, although the latter was around a mile and a half away. (Norfolk Railway Society)

106. As at Hainault, the tracks serving Fairlop station were on embankment, although the platforms and buildings were supported on arches. The signal box, which stood at the north end of the site, accommodated a twenty-eight lever McKenzie & Holland frame and functioned from 1903 until 20th April 1948. Behind this, but not visible in the photograph, was the goods yard, which included a cattle dock and three-ton crane. A 1930s plan to develop a civilian airport beside the line would have resulted in the station being rebuilt about 500yds to the south, but the scheme failed to materialise. (Lens of Sutton collection)

107. After closure of the signal box a power operated ground frame was installed to control access to and from the goods yard, but the yard closed from 24th March 1958 and the frame was presumably rendered redundant. Apart from this, the station remained little altered since GER days although its awnings were shortened at the north end, as is apparent in this view which shows a train of 1962 Stock departing for Hainault in the 1980s. (J.L. Crook)

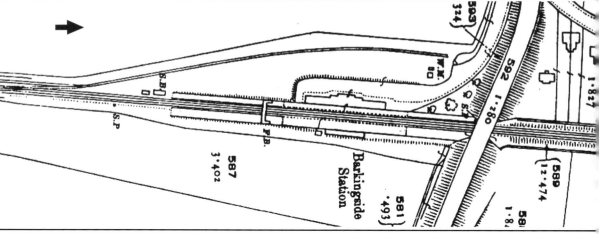

Barkingside, located 5miles from Woodford, again consisted of two platforms and followed the same pattern as we have encountered before in that it was accompanied by a stationmaster's house and six semi-detached cottages for the other members of staff. These can be seen near the top right of this Ordnance Survey extract from 1919, whilst to the left lies the single road goods yard.

108. The exterior featured more in the way of architectural embellishment than the other stations along the line, possibly because it was close to Dr. Barnado's Village Home For Girls, which was patronised by Royalty. This photograph was taken around the time of opening and includes the twenty-four lever McKenzie & Holland-built signalbox to the right, which remained in use until March 1948. (Norfolk Railway Society)

116. Looking south from Eastern Avenue in the following decade, we see a train of 1962 Stock heading towards Hainault. The tube lines were laid either side of the existing LNER formation, with tunnels at the southern end. After closure to freight traffic in 1956, the rails towards Seven Kings were lifted, but, as the remaining Hainault Loop goods trains required reversing facilities, LT laid a run-round siding on the old trackbed. Goods workings ceased in 1965, but the facility was retained for the use of LT engineers' trains and was not abandoned until 16th August 1992. (C.D. Connor)

117. We end our journey over the original GER Hainault Loop, with this view taken from the Vicarage Lane overbridge in 1936. Between Newbury Park station and here there were three other bridges; the first was unused, but lay near the east end of Brancaster Road. The second carried Wards Road and the third was Benton Road. Near the centre of our photograph stands the twenty-eight lever McKenzie & Holland-built Newbury Park Junction signal box, which opened in 1903 and remained in use until late 1947. As indicated on the original print, the tracks on the left led to Seven Kings, whilst those to the right served Ilford. The passenger service towards Ilford was withdrawn from 30th November 1947, but the freight link with Seven Kings lasted until 19th March 1956. Photographs of the two junctions with the main line may be found in the Middleton Press volume *Ilford to Shenfield* by Dave Brennand. (British Rail)

# THE UNDERGROUND CONNECTION

Now that we have finished our exploration of the ex-GER Stratford-Ongar and Hainault Loop lines, we must take a brief look at the section of route which provides a direct link between Newbury Park and Leytonstone. The majority of this is located in tunnel and was, of course, built as part of the 1935-40 New Works Plan.

Contracts for its construction were let during the closing years of the 1930s and much had been completed when wartime conditions brought progress to a halt.

The unfinished tunnels proved particularly useful however, as part of them was fitted out as a factory, providing 300,000 square feet of accommodation for the Plessey Company which was engaged in manufacturing aircraft parts essential to the war effort. Work on the conversion started towards the end of 1940 and was completed in March 1942. To enable more efficient movement of materials and finished components, each tunnel was provided with an 18in gauge railway track.

After hostilities ended, the factory was dismantled and its former location eventually reverted to its intended purpose, with the line opening to public traffic on 14th December 1947.

118. Heading west from Newbury Park we come to Gants Hill, which is located beneath the intersection of Eastern Avenue, Woodford Avenue and Cranbrook Road. This station, which was designed by Adams, Holden & Pearson, was referred to on the original plans as 'North Ilford', but the name changed prior to opening. Construction started in 1937 and it was brought into use ten years later. The ticket hall was located under the intersection roundabout and its entrance from street level was to have been distinguished by a prominent clocktower, but this was never built. Down below, a pair of MY-type escalators, with a rise of 32ft 3ins, led down to a 150ft long concourse, with a 20ft high vaulted roof based on a design previously used on the Moscow Metro. From here passageways led to the two platforms, which were clad in biscuit coloured tiling, lined out with chrome yellow bands. A third escalator, similar to the others, was brought into use on 14th March 1948 and the concourse, which had partially opened in an unfinished state, was opened fully three weeks later on 4th April. This view, which includes a train of 1962 Stock, also shows the type of tiled name frieze used at certain stations during the immediate pre and postwar periods. (J.E. Connor)

119. The earliest plans for Redbridge station are thought to date from late 1935, when it was proposed as *'West Ilford'*. The name was subsequently changed to *'Red House'* after a nearby hostelry, then Red Bridge, which was initially shown as two words but subsequently combined into one. No work had been carried out on the street level building before the war and construction was hampered by the need to remove facilities connected with the Plessey factory. A start was eventually made in 1946, but steel shortages resulted in further delays and the building remained unfinished until the final months of 1948. The platforms are only about 16 feet below the surface, so the station tunnels were constructed by the cut and cover method. As this photograph shows, the tiled frieze here does not include the name, but features a succession of LT bullseye symbols. (J.E. Connor)

120. We now arrive at Wanstead, which is the final station on our tour. As can be seen the platform tunnels are similar to those at Gants Hill and the tiled friezes include the name. West of here trains continue to Leytonstone, where they rejoin the former GER route and continue into central London. (J.E. Connor)

# MP Middleton Press
## EVOLVING THE ULTIMATE RAIL ENCYCLOPEDIA

Easebourne Lane, Midhurst, West Sussex.
GU29 9AZ   Tel:01730 813169

www.middletonpress.co.uk   email:info@middletonpress.co.uk
A-0 906520   B-1 873793   C-1 901706   D-1 904474

OOP Out of print at time of printing - Please check availability   BROCHURE AVAILABLE SHOWING NEW TITLES